P9-CEV-340

Country Style

TIME-LIFE BOOKS

Alexandria, Virginia

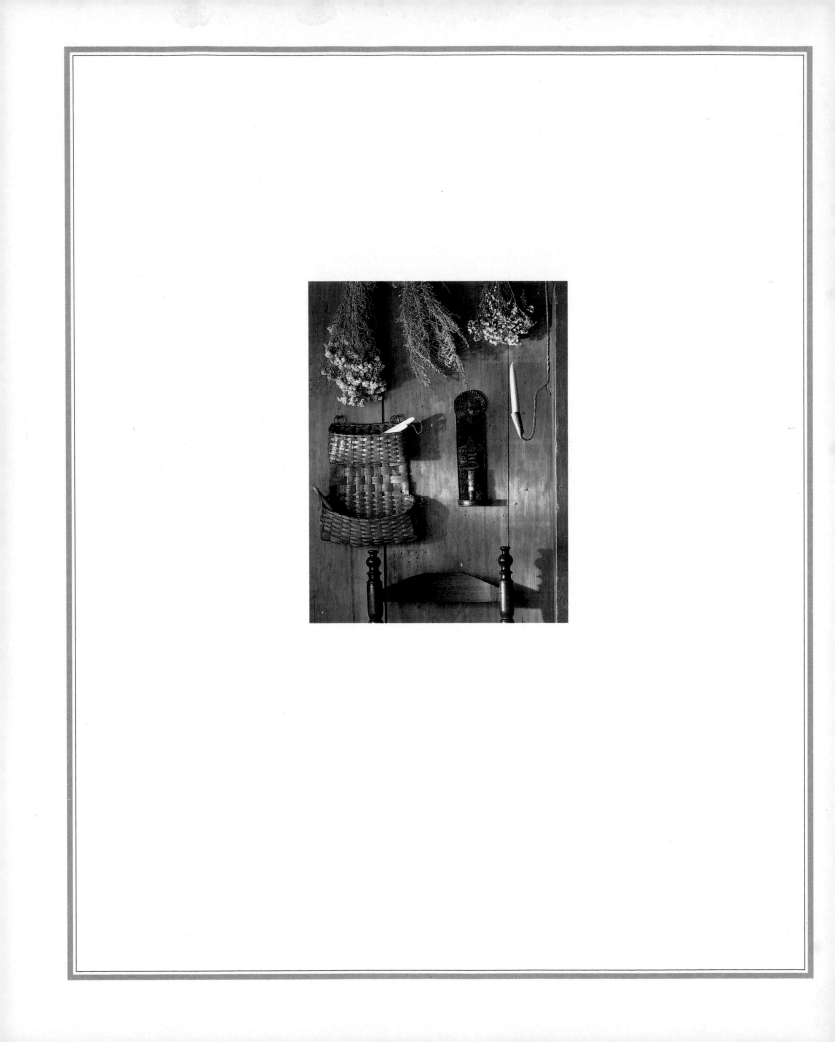

Country Style

four distinctive looks
for decorating a
country home

A REBUS BOOK

C O N T E N T S

INTRODUCTION

6

Traditional

Romantic

Formal

Casual

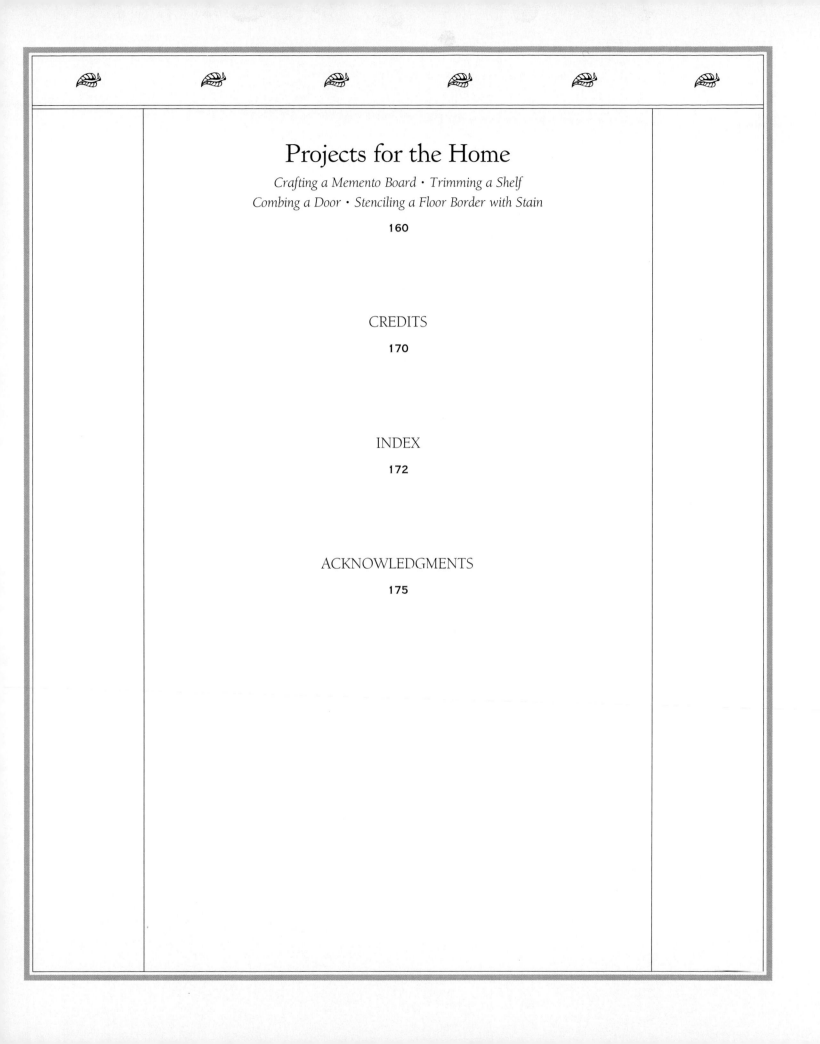

Projects for the Home

Crafting a Memento Board · Trimming a Shelf
Combing a Door · Stenciling a Floor Border with Stain

160

P erhaps the greatest appeal of country style is the broad range of interpretations that are possible. This volume explores four of the most popular country looks—traditional, romantic, formal, and casual—and defines the furniture types, fabrics, decorations, and accessories that contribute to each. A traditional look, for example, might incorporate early American antiques and homespun fabrics, while a romantic approach tends toward wicker and chintz. A formal country decor is usually carefully coordinated, whereas a casual country style is shaped by the idea that "anything goes."

Understanding the essentials of the different styles, however, is only the beginning, since how you choose to interpret country style will ultimately depend on individual taste. While all of the houses featured in this book show the care and time spent on them, not all of the homeowners had a specific decorating plan in mind when they started. As you will see, a serendipitous approach to renovation and decorating can be as successful as one that is more studied.

In every one of the twelve houses shown on the following pages, the homeowners have personalized the decor, adapting ideas from the past and present to their own needs. Often, the overall effect extends beyond the interior furnishings to an interest in the architectural features of a house. Many of the families who renovated older homes, for instance, have devoted long hours to research in local libraries, town halls, historical societies, and museums, where they unearthed deeds, photographs, and other records that might provide clues to the original appearance of their houses.

Great pains were then taken to restore both the exteriors and interiors to look as they would have when the buildings were originally erected. In some cases the owners were able to recover original architectural elements from the houses themselves; pediments were found stored in attics or basements, original paneling was uncovered after ripping out new walls. In houses where the details had long been destroyed, the owners replaced them with pieces rescued from old buildings slated for demolition or with elements purchased through companies specializing in architectural salvage. And in many instances, family members enjoyed rolling up their shirt sleeves and doing the physical work themselves: stripping woodwork of accumulated paint, sanding down floors, or trying their hand at decorative stenciling.

It is precisely because country decorating allows such personal involvement that it is so popular today. With that in mind, the last chapter of this book includes directions for four projects for the home. By decorating with pieces that you have made yourself, you are assured of establishing a country look that is entirely your own.

Traditional

*a classic, timeless style
that reflects a strong sense
of history*

❧

An unpretentious approach to country decorating, the traditional look finds inspiration in the past, favoring the types of furnishings that would have been used in early American houses. Here you will find classic wing chairs, sturdy Windsors, and well-worn banister-backs. Simple homespun and gingham curtains drape windows, while rag rugs warm wide-board floors. Vintage baskets and clusters of dried flowers might hang from the beams in a homey keeping room. And every mantelpiece proudly displays a collection—of pewter, perhaps, or country pottery.

In this flexible decorating style, both antiques and reproductions are equally at home. Two of the houses shown in this chapter are furnished with 18th- and 19th-century pieces that the owners have spent years collecting. A third house, however, is filled with newly crafted pieces—made by the owner's hand. Indeed, old, new, or a mix of both is appropriate, as long as the overall effect is simple, welcoming, and "true to tradition."

*Classic American furnishings, like this wing chair and 18th-century tea table, help
create a traditional feeling in a country parlor.*

Farmhouse Style

The mural in the stairwell above was commissioned by the homeowners as a tribute to the countryside surrounding their midwestern farmhouse. The contemporary artist who created it models her work after that of 19th-century itinerant painters, called limners.

This 19th-century midwestern farmhouse is considered by its owners to be the finest "antique" in their collection, and they have treated it with the sensitivity befitting such a treasure. The couple discovered the rare stone farmhouse in an area where all the other homes were either brick or frame. They were particularly drawn to its setting amid hundreds of unspoiled acres. "This house really takes you back in time," says one of the owners, "because you don't see anything around it but hills and valleys."

While the homeowners felt that the location was perfect, the building itself was not. Erected in the 1830s, the house was structurally sound but in need of a great deal of interior renovation. To obtain background information, the owners, experienced restorers, undertook extensive research on 19th-century design at libraries and museums. The resulting work maintains period authenticity while incorporating the owners' personal tastes. For color and pattern on the stairwell walls, for example, they added a contemporary mural depicting the house and surrounding farmstead, but had it done in the style of a 19th-century itinerant limner. Old

Continued

10

The owners painted the woodwork in the entryway and stairwell at left a soft taupe color; adapted from a similar hue used by 19th-century Shakers, it complements the muted colors of the mural. At the top of the stairs is a "portrait" of the stone house, and in the hall, a harbor scene that alludes to the homeowners' love of sailing.

Above, an 18th-century cherry candlestand and ox-yoke banister-back chair—both bearing their original finish—are typical of the traditional furnishings found throughout the house.

wallpaper was carefully scraped off in downstairs rooms and the woodwork stripped to uncover the original paint. Rather than match the gray and blue colors that they found, the owners chose subdued taupe tones.

When the removal of old carpeting and linoleum in the downstairs rooms revealed the original chestnut boards, the couple decided to leave the floor natural; in the upstairs rooms, however, they painted the floors a tan shade for a

Continued

In the parlor at right, accessories include an 1831 leather fire bucket on the hearth and a bowl of old stone fruit on an antique gate-leg table.

The two stone fireplaces in the keeping room at right are original to the house. The one on the left was once used for heating and baking, and the one on the right was for everyday cooking. Both are outfitted with 18th- and 19th-century iron and tin cooking utensils, including broilers and trivets. The sink between the fireplaces, signed and dated 1840, is made of stone, and was added by the owners.

The salt-glazed stoneware crock above was made in the 1800s by a pottery in New Geneva, Pennsylvania. The eagle and shield are typical stenciled motifs. Once used for storing food, such crocks make attractive accessories today.

*Traditional open shelving
and a vintage butcher-shop
meat rack provide storage
in the kitchen, right. A
collection of redware is
displayed on the scalloped
pine shelves, and antique
kitchen utensils hang from
the iron rack. The red-
painted flour bin dates
from the 1800s.*

warmer feeling. A collection of rag rugs, canvas floor cloths, and Oriental carpets provides additional color throughout the house.

The owners became so attuned to a traditional 19th-century look that they knew instinctively when to recycle antique household fixtures and furnishings, when to renovate, and when to use reproductions. Upon discovering an original parlor mantelpiece and cupboard in the attic, they restored them and returned them to their rightful places. A "modern" kitchen was replaced with a comfortable keeping room that better suited the rustic character of the house —the refrigerator was concealed behind cabinetry and other appliances were hidden in an

Continued

The 19th-century bucket bench above was once used to store water pails, pitchers, and other washing utensils. Today it is stocked with period kitchenware such as swivel-handled firkins and a heart-shaped tin cheese strainer. A mechanical apple parer hangs above the bench.

The 19th-century clothes chest, low-post bed, and potato-stamped blanket chest above are among the traditional pieces in the guest room.

alcove. Combining their aesthetic ideals with practical needs, they chose several quality replicas of 19th-century candle fixtures that are equipped with ingeniously hidden electrical wires.

While the owners were intent on a period look, they nevertheless wanted to avoid a museumlike atmosphere, and did so by using favorite furnishings and collectibles in each room. Avid sailors, they placed nautical memorabilia, including a ship model, a marine painting, and a brass telescope, throughout the house. The 18th- and 19th-century American furniture they have been collecting for fifteen years reflect their individual taste. Their pieces include finely turned banister-back and ladder-back chairs, and painted pieces such as a potato-stamped blanket chest and a paneled wardrobe. "I knew from the moment I saw it that I wanted early American furniture in our home," says one of the owners. "But I also knew I didn't want it just for show. I had to be able to use it."

To bring a feeling of warmth to the guest room, the owners had a colorful border stenciled on the walls at left and added a brightly painted paneled wardrobe. Textiles were used as accents. While the boy's clothing, hand-woven shawl, and homespun blanket draped over the chair are antiques, the linen bedspread, with a tree of life motif worked in crewel, was made by a contemporary craftswoman.

Antique furniture and accessories in the master bedroom at left include an 18th-century tiger maple chest of drawers; the acorn-finial bed and the chalkware figurines on the mantel and shelves are from the 19th century. The wood-slat blinds and crewelwork curtains are contemporary interpretations of 19th-century window treatments.

TURKISH CARPETS IN THE COLONIES

Robert Feke's 1741 portrait *Isaac Royall and His Family*, above, depicts a Turkish-made Transylvanian Church carpet.

Oriental rugs were a rare luxury in colonial America, and were found only in the households of the wealthy. Until the middle of the 18th century, the traditional use for these exotic carpets—which provided color and texture in rooms that were otherwise quite austere—was not on floors, but draped over tables or chests; the valuable textiles were thus protected from wear.

Virtually all Oriental carpets in colonial America were made in Turkey. Distinguished by their hand-knotted pile, they were usually in one of two designs: Medallion Ushak, characterized by a central medallion, or the double-arch Transylvanian Church pattern (so called because these carpets were found in Balkan churches, where they were placed as votive offerings).

Turkey was one of the few countries in the East that was accessible to European sea trade in the 17th and 18th centuries. Relatively scarce, Turkish carpets came via England to colonial America, where they were generally purchased through importers, in shops, or at auction. The carpets were also occasionally acquired directly by individuals making voyages to the mother country. One notable American, Benjamin Franklin, selected a Turkish carpet at the request of his wife while he was on a trip to London in 1765. Franklin sent home "A Large true Turkey Carpet cost 10 Guineas, for the Dining Parlour."

Although no Turkish carpets have survived from the colonial period, they are found listed in household inventories and wills. One of the earliest references appears in the 1673 will of one Elizabeth Butler of Virginia, in an entry that notes a "drawing table and Turkey carpet."

Oriental carpets are also depicted in a few American paintings of the day. Robert Feke's 1741 portrait *Isaac Royall and His Family,* above, features a "Turkey Carpitt" as a table cover. The luxurious textile is a fitting symbol of the prominent station of Royall, a successful New England rum merchant.

This 19th-century "Turkey Carpitt" displays the Medallion Ushak pattern.

A Transylvanian Church carpet features the typical double-arch design.

Tradition Restored

The New England colonial house shown here was built as a saltbox by a town selectman in 1720, and enlarged as a parsonage in the 1790s and early 1800s for a Yale-educated minister. It has been meticulously restored by its present owners, who still consider it a work in progress. Indeed, the family feel that they are "caretakers" of the house and are researching every step of its restoration. "We're trying to help the house be what it *should* be," says one of the owners, "not just what we want it to be."

Among their first efforts was extensive work on the exterior, which featured many of the original clapboards and handwrought iron rose-head nails, so named for the shape of their heads. While the house was basically sound when the couple bought it, it was in need of a new roof (they chose hand-split cedar shakes in keeping with the period) and attention to the 1800s porch addition, which was sagging and pulling away from the main structure. Jacking up the porch and adding a stone foundation solved that problem, but consequently caused some of the plaster walls and ceilings inside the house to crumble.

This led to work on the interior, including restoration of each room. Says one of the owners, "The most outstanding attribute of the house is that no one has changed it structurally

Continued

Many of the 18th-century clapboards on the house at right are original, but the paint color is not. The owners plan to restore the early red-brown color.

The 18th-century pine paneling in the entryway above was carefully angled to fit the stairwell; in restoration the woodwork was painted to match traces of the original blue-green paint.

over the years." Indeed, they discovered that much of the early woodwork, flooring, and decorative detailing was still intact, although partially hidden. In the sitting room, for example, wallpaper covered sophisticated stenciled patterns that were probably painted in the 1830s, when a prominent physician lived in the house. The swag-and-tassel pattern, large circular medallions, vine border, and other motifs have now been restored to their original colors —red and green—by a contemporary artist. The owners also spent hundreds of hours stripping paint from the entryway and stairwell, revealing the original blue-green woodwork, which they then repainted to match. The pine-board steps and random-width flooring have been given a natural finish.

The entry hall is one of three areas in the

Continued

Because the plaster walls had cracked, the original stenciled patterns in the sitting room at left had to be re-created on new plaster. Appropriate furnishings for this elegant room include a ball-footed chest made in Connecticut between 1680 and 1720.

house featuring raised, or fielded, paneling, a relatively expensive wall treatment used in colonial times. Such formal paneling befits a house in which prominent community leaders once lived. In the parlor, one of the areas now used for dining, the panels had once been painted, then later stripped and waxed. The owners gently removed the wax, revealing the natural patina of aged wood. Here, the paneling makes a handsome backdrop for two prized pieces of furniture—an imposing burl walnut highboy and a carved dower chest from around the late 1600s—as well as several rare brass candlesticks dating to the 16th and 17th centuries.

Continued

The parlor at left is furnished with banister-back chairs and a gate-leg table from the 1700s. A 19th-century tin candle fixture hangs overhead.

Near the fireplace in the parlor, an 18th-century birch stand with a bird's-eye maple drawer, above, displays a bell metal pitcher and glassware from the 1700s. Behind the stand, a storage cupboard built into the original paneling features 18th-century butterfly hinges.

Simpler pine paneling adorns the fireplace wall in the old kitchen. Now used as a family room, it boasts one of five original fireplaces in the house. Here, the walk-in fireplace had been walled over and fitted with a wood-burning stove; once the fireplace was uncovered, the original crane was found in place and now displays a collection of hearth-cooking utensils, including skimmers, trivets, ladles, frying pans, and a pair of rare 17th-century andirons with spit racks.

In addition to small antique decorative objects, early American furniture carefully selected over the course of twenty-five years brings a distinctive traditional look to each room. Included are a number of finely carved banister-back chairs and gate-leg tables, which were both common furniture forms in the 1700s. The homeowners have become particularly interested in the provenance of their antique furnishings, and they cherish one chair in the parlor especially for its intriguing inscription. Inked on a small piece of linen that has been sewn to the underside of the rush seat, the message reads, "This chair was a part of the wedding outfit of Mary Porter, daughter of Rev. John Porter of North Bridgewater, who married Rev. Thomas Crafts December 28, 1786."

In the old kitchen above, candlelight casts a warm glow. The collection of candleholders — which date from the 16th to the 19th centuries — includes tin lanterns and sconces, brass candlesticks, and a simple chandelier with wrought-iron arms.

In the dining area opposite, the owners preserved the period look by installing salvaged eight-over-twelve windows and a pine door with its original strap hinges.

31

Moses Eaton, Stenciler

Moses Eaton, Jr., was one of the most prolific itinerant stencilers of the early 19th century. At a time when wallpaper was affordable to only the wealthy, Eaton offered an alternative: fashionable painted decoration in exchange for bed, board, and a modest fee.

The son of Moses Eaton, Sr., a Revolutionary War soldier and stenciler himself, the artist was born in 1796 in Hancock, New Hampshire, and lived to the age of ninety in a nearby town. A successful farmer, Eaton also traveled throughout Maine, Massachusetts, and his home state decorating houses and taverns, roughly between 1814 and the 1840s. The exact number of interiors stenciled by his hand is unknown; painted around 1825, the plaster wall fragment from a Maine home above is one of the few examples positively identified as Eaton's work. But many painted stencil patterns are attributed to him—or to other early stencilers who copied his designs.

In the 1930s, Eaton's stenciling kit was found in the attic of his sister's home. The small wooden box contained at least fifty stencils he had cut from heavy paper; the motifs include simple leaves, geometric shapes, swags and tassels, and an intricate pineapple. The oft-used stencils, some of which are shown at right, bear traces of the paints that Eaton— and, no doubt, his color-hungry customers—favored, including red, green, coral, and ocher. Also in the box were brushes, chalk and string (used for measuring), and the powdered pigments that Eaton mixed with milk and oil to make paint. It was with these modest tools and materials—a tiny, portable workshop— that Eaton produced his bold designs, still admired and copied today.

Colonial Inspiration

After visiting an 18th-century center-hall house in Connecticut, the owners of this contemporary colonial in the Western Reserve region of Ohio knew exactly the type of home they wanted to build. Their motivations were both historical and personal.

Because the Western Reserve was a territory of Connecticut until 1800, and settled almost exclusively by easterners, New England-style houses are common in the area. And since one of the homeowners crafts Windsor chairs, the family wanted a proper setting for his work.

Continued

Simple furnishings chosen to complement the handcrafted Windsor chairs in the parlor include the reproduction camelback sofa, left, and the circa 1800 "dishtop" candlestand, above.

In the spacious dining room at right, the seven-foot-long tiger maple harvest table and the Windsor chairs—including the bow-backs around the table, a child's highchair, and two continuous-arm comb-backs—were made by the home-owner. An antique rag rug, muslin tab curtains, and blue-gray wood trim contribute to the traditional feeling of the room.

Built on a plot of the family farm, the house was designed and constructed by the owners themselves with trees from their property. Wood from the farm was also used for the Windsor chairs that are found throughout the house; the owners do not consider these chairs "reproductions" but, rather, fine pieces—made almost three hundred years after the appearance of the earliest English prototypes. The chairs are fashioned with hand-whittled spindles, hand-turned legs, and knuckles carved with tools that the craftsman inherited from his grandfather.

Such respect for the past, coupled with a practical approach to the present, is evident everywhere in the house. "Sometimes we were torn between authenticity and our own needs," says

Continued

To create an 18th-century country look in the keeping room, hand-planed poplar boards were used
for the walls and cupboards, left, and for the simple paneled cabinets, above.

one of the owners, "so occasionally we would be forced to compromise." For example, the house was framed with extra-wide studs that permitted deep, large windows; while such windows were not typical in the 18th century, the homeowners decided to use them because they open up the house to sunlight and permit better views of the farm. The couple also installed plank flooring, which is naturally finished, throughout the house; it not only adds a period look, but is also easy to maintain. Crown molding, chair rails, boxed beams, and peg racks—

Continued

Among the antiques in the master bedroom is the portrait above, which depicts a great-great-great-grandfather of one of the owners. The bed at right displays a 19th-century coverlet.

The homeowner made the miniature writing-arm Windsor chair above as a Christmas gift for his wife. All of its features, including the comb back and the scrolled ears and knuckles, were handcrafted using full-size tools.

all painted in traditional colors—are other decorative touches that lend character to the new house.

In addition to being true to colonial traditions, the homeowners also enjoy displaying their family heirlooms, many of which reflect a Scandinavian heritage. The polychrome wooden roosters and a child's trestle table in the guest room, for example, were inherited from Swedish ancestors. Other simple accessories such as traditional tab curtains and hand-sewn bed linens also complement this eclectic collection of furnishings.

The Jacob's Ladder quilt on the rope bed in the guest room at right is an heirloom, as is the child's Swedish trestle table.

Antique toys can bring a whimsical sense of the past to any room of the house. The pottery bank above was made in England and is inscribed "Mary Ann West, Lodge Green, Meriden, Warwickshire, October 1849." Such 19th-century banks featured a single slot—this one is in the chimney—but no easy "exit" for the carefully saved coins.

IN THE WINDSOR STYLE

Windsor furniture is characterized by individual elements—turned legs and spindles—radiating from a plank "hub," such as a seat or tabletop. Instead of being joined by a mortise and tenon or other traditional technique, the pieces are tightly socketed together. The most common furniture forms made in this manner are side chairs and armchairs; in fact, in the 18th and early 19th centuries, sturdy, comfortable Windsor chairs were among the most popular furnishings in English and American homes.

Yet these chairs were not the only furniture to feature the separate stick-like "parts" and socket construction; Windsor chair makers also adapted the style to a variety of forms, as shown by the pieces at right. The shaped plank seat, for instance, found its way onto rockers, highchairs, stools, and chair-tables. The spindles, and the curved crest rails that hold them, were used on settees, day beds, cribs, and cradles. And the turned legs and stretchers appeared on tables and stands.

Windsor chairs were also modified—sometimes years after their manufacture—into different forms. Some were fitted with rockers; another innovative hybrid was a chair surmounted by a foot-powered fan.

Continuous-arm settee with bamboo turnings, 1790-1810

Candlestand, Pennsylvania, 1750-1780; original green paint

Fan chair, New York, 1780-1790; original yellow paint

Sack-back highchair, Massachusetts, 1800-1810

Footstool, New York City, c. 1790

Bow-back armchair with applied rockers, c. 1900

Chair-table, late 1700s to early 1800s

Romantic

old-fashioned comfort
touched with a sense
of nostalgia

There is no single definition of the romantic country look: it might be clean and simple, a jumble of accessories, or quaintly Victorian. Yet, while the houses shown on the following pages reflect a variety of tastes and decorating solutions, they all share certain characteristics. Evident in each home is a rich sense of color and pattern. Rooms are light, airy, cozy, and comfortable — the walls covered in a pretty floral-print paper, perhaps, or trimmed with a lively painted border. Fabrics tend to be brightly patterned chintzes, while framed botanicals, dainty lace pillows, and dried-flower arrangements are the accessories of choice.

To achieve this fresh country look, a free-spirited approach is essential. Flea-market finds are at home with family heirlooms, and serious period pieces usually take second place to furniture that is old, well-loved, and easy to live with. Above all, an inviting character, intended to make friends and family feel welcome, is readily apparent in a romantic country home.

A rose theme repeated in the chintz wallcovering and other fabrics, as well as in the rug
and the accessories, sets a romantic tone in a guest bedroom.

A Victorian Retreat

Originally built in the 1870s as a summer home for the Tiffany family, the house shown here and on the following pages is one of the few examples of the Victorian Carpenter Gothic style in its Long Island, New York, community. Trimmed with "gingerbread" fretwork and featuring Gothic-arched windows, the house looks just as romantic today as it did in the days when it was first constructed.

The present owner, an interior designer from New York City who uses the house on weekends, had long been familiar with the property (a landmark in the area) when it came up for sale some years ago. "I was already very taken with the architecture of the house and with the setting," he says, "but I had never seen what the inside looked like." When he did finally view the interior, he found it gloomy—the walls were covered with brown and purple wallpaper and

Continued

White-painted wicker chairs on the verandah above provide comfortable seating near an unusual Dutch door. The glass-paned section of the door slides up like a window, and the lower section swings inward.

Victorian Carpenter Gothic houses, such as the one opposite built in the 1870s, frequently had several different roof lines, as well as lacy roof edging, fretwork, and Gothic-arched windows.

French doors, which lead outside, and a mix of floral chintzes create a garden-like feeling in the versatile living room at right.

there were three layers of dark curtains at every window. The exterior, including the trim and brackets, was also quite forbidding, painted a dark red that the owner felt did not suit the whimsical style of the house. "Structurally, the house was in excellent condition," he says, "but the decor presented a challenge. I wanted to bring it back to a state of beauty."

Dubbing the house Rose Hall, he enlivened the clapboard exterior with rose-colored paint and blue-gray trim—choosing contrasting colors to emphasize the fanciful details. Inside, the original well-proportioned spaces were left intact. No walls were removed, but French doors were added in the living room to open

Continued

*In the dining room, a French console and mirror
are mixed with an English table and chairs.*

*A colorful chintz with a pale
yellow background covers
the dining room walls,
giving the room a sunny
look. The green-and-
white trompe l'oeil wall-
paper below the chair
rail resembles a formal
porch railing.*

Known as delftware, pieces such as the colander-bowl above take their name from the town of Delft in Holland. Such tin-glazed earthenware was produced in this Dutch pottery center and in England during the 17th century to compete with the importation of expensive Chinese porcelain. Highly collectible today, delftware makes pretty decoration in any room of the house.

onto the terrace and gardens. White paint was used to bring out the crisp lines of door and window moldings, as well as stairway banisters that were obscured by dark stain and varnish. The original inlaid marble-and-soapstone mantelpieces still in place in each room were refurbished, and Victorian lighting fixtures (which the new owner converted from gas to electricity) were installed to enhance the authentic look.

The interior was completely redecorated in warm pastels and in patterns that share a rose motif. A variety of chintzes were used not only for curtains and furniture upholstery but also for the walls. "Upholstering" walls was a time-consuming technique, the homeowner admits, but one that gave the rooms a softer and more luxurious look than wallpaper could. "I don't like hard edges in a house," he explains. "Rooms should be inviting, so that you sink right into them. Colors and fabrics are essential in creating

Continued

To add elegance to the downstairs bathroom, above and opposite, the owner converted a Victorian commode into a sink counter and installed an elaborate 19th-century cranberry-glass ceiling lamp.

A draped valance and rose-patterned chintzes give the guest bedroom above a singularly romantic feeling. Pillows covered in antique linens and lace and clustered on the Victorian iron-and-brass bed contribute to the inviting look of the room.

that feeling. I don't think a house can ever be successful if it isn't comfortable."

The homeowner did not concern himself with decorating the house in strict period style, choosing instead to combine Victorian furniture with earlier 19th-century French and English pieces, as well as furnishings from the 1930s and 1940s. His goal was an interior that would look gently used, not newly redone, with a mix of furnishings that created the feeling of a Victorian country home.

The ample size of the house also offers plenty

of room for houseguests and entertaining. The dining room, for instance, accommodates fourteen. It contains the most formal furniture in the house and provides a setting for the owner's collection of antique porcelain and crystal. Less formal meals are enjoyed at a massive pine table in the sunny, all-purpose living room.

Always ready for visitors, six bedrooms on the upper two floors of the house look out onto the luxurious branches of enormous oak and chestnut trees. Outfitted with antique beds and dressers, these rooms, like those downstairs, of-

fer a substantial degree of comfort. The use of floral chintzes and harmonious colors is also prevalent, yet each room retains a distinct personality, achieved in part through the use of different window treatments. Some of the bedrooms have Gothic-arched windows, requiring clever arrangement of the draperies. In one bedroom, abutting windows are of different heights: the designer solved the problem with a gently draped valance centered above the tallest window and caught by three fabric rosettes. In a third-story bedroom (overleaf), tucked in

under the sloping roof, the windows were so nicely framed by trees that he added no curtains at all, but simply painted the moldings white. Complemented by the painted floor and furniture, the unaffected window treatment helps to give the room the cozy look of an old-fashioned attic bedroom.

In summing up his feelings about the house, the owner remarks, "I love this house because there is a sense of magic to it. It's the most romantic house I've ever been in, but at the same time it really is just a nice, old country place."

In keeping with the Carpenter Gothic style of the house, the homeowner trimmed the pale yellow walls of the bedroom above with a wallpaper border in a Gothic arch pattern. The carved walnut bed was made in France in the 19th century.

Painted furniture adds to the old-fashioned feeling of the bedroom at right. The green Austrian cupboard, built into one wall, has enameled porcelain panels. The yellow Scandinavian blanket chest dates from the 19th century.

Cast-iron doorstops, such as the setter above, were widely used in America from the late 1800s until the mid-20th century. Manufactured by foundries throughout the Midwest, such pieces were produced from molds and then painted by hand. Flowers are among the most common form of doorstop; dogs and other animals are far more rare.

spandrel

baluster

brackets

grille

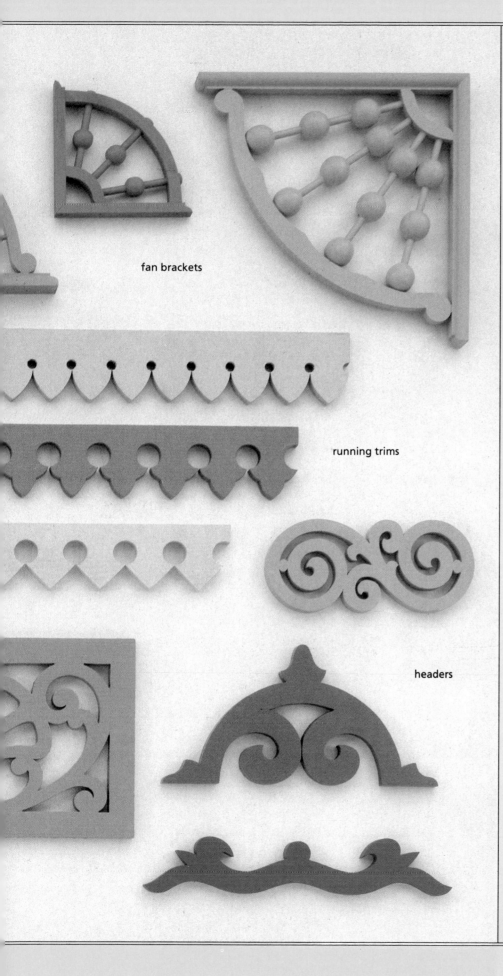

fan brackets

running trims

headers

GINGERBREAD TRIM

One of the most distinctive architectural legacies of 19th-century America is "gingerbread": the ornamental wood brackets, balusters, and trims closely associated with the Carpenter Gothic cottages of the mid- to late 1800s. The Carpenter Gothic style has its roots in the simple cottage plans published in books by Andrew Jackson Downing, an influential architecture critic of the time. Carpenters throughout the country made use of his pattern books, interpreting the popular designs as they saw fit; hence the name Carpenter Gothic.

Also at their disposal was a new-found supply of gingerbread trim. Wood was plentiful, and the invention of the power-driven jigsaw around 1840 made it possible to cut an endless variety of shapes from the inexpensive material. Lacy wooden trims could be mail-ordered by the yard from the factories where they were mass-produced. These readily available architectural elements provided an affordable alternative to the costly carved stone decoration found on grander Gothic architecture of the same period.

Gingerbread is still available from woodworking companies, and can be used to restore a period Carpenter Gothic cottage, or to help trim a new house. Among the pieces at left are spandrels for trimming doorways, fan brackets for roofs, and flat-cut balusters for porch railings.

Seaside
Comfort

The New Jersey house, originally built in the 1890s as a cottage on a larger estate, was doubled in size early in this century to serve as a full-scale home. Large rooms, ample porches for outdoor dining and summertime sleeping, and a handsomely landscaped yard give the residence a generous sense of comfort that suits the busy family of four that live here. "All of these things are real luxuries that our whole family enjoy," says one homeowner. In fact, the house was so well loved by its previous owners that when this couple purchased it, they

found that they were only the third family to live there.

While the current owners were initially attracted to the appealing exterior and romantic seaside setting of the house, its overall layout also offered many assets. The house is situated so that each room receives some natural light during the day and offers attractive views of gardens, trees, and lawns. The floor plans, which are designed around central hallways, add to the feeling of space and privacy.

When the couple first moved in, the house

Continued

Located near the ocean and two large rivers, the New Jersey house at left was used as a summer cottage before it became a year-round home. Porches on each side of the house still make it ideal for summertime living.

Made in Europe and America
during the second half of the
19th century, majolica
tableware was immensely
popular during the Victorian
era. Decorated with
lustrous, lead-base glazes, the
pottery was often molded
in naturalistic shapes,
including animals, vege-
tables, and birds such as
the owl above.

needed a great deal of work, but because they did not want the restoration to overwhelm them, they chose to undertake the project in stages. The most immediate problem was the exterior. First, the owners had the old paint removed, leaving the original decorative shingle patterns in place. The shingles were then stained to a weathered gray that suits the house's location near the shore. Next, the shutters were taken off and the windows and trim repainted. "We quickly discovered that there are two hundred and six windows," one homeowner says. "The trims alone provided more than enough work."

Indoors, the rooms were immediately painted,

Continued

Among the homeowners' favorite accessories are prints, pottery, and enameled boxes—like those on the living room table above—with the themes of flowers, fruit, and animals. A majolica cabbage-leaf plate and a botanical print paired together by a taffeta ribbon make a particularly decorative display.

At left, the oak floor in the living room has been painted to resemble tiles, and the coffee table and fireplace bricks are marbleized.

Complementing a collection of garden-theme pottery, the woodwork and cupboards · in the dining room at right are painted with a green marble finish. When the room is used for special dinners and family gatherings, the table is dressed with a triple layer of tablecloths.

In the sitting room, also
used as an office, floral motifs
are offset by a checkerboard
theme that is repeated in the
hooked rug, woven wicker
chairs, and throw.

to make them more livable; the completed decor, however, evolved over the course of several years. Although the family's previous house was also large, this one seemed to swallow up their furniture. "The rooms didn't look very big when we first stepped inside," says one homeowner, "but as soon as we began to fill them with furniture we realized how huge they are. In part, it's the high ceilings that create that large scale." One of their primary concerns in decorating the house was to transform these lofty spaces into warm, inviting, and comfortable places for family activities and entertaining.

One of the homeowners, a professional decorator, brought both imagination and skill to the task, using color and pattern to give the house a cozy feeling and a unified appearance. In some rooms, she started with a particular fabric that she loved, and developed the color scheme around it. In the dining room and small living

Continued

Pink walls overbrushed with white, above, provide a soft, warm background for a display of botanical prints, plates, and other treasures.

room, which are linked by a large arched doorway, she used the same fabric. Painting the walls and woodwork in these rooms in different but compatible colors also helped to create a subtle visual connection.

She also used a wide variety of chintzes throughout the house, gathering generous lengths of yardage into luxurious curtains that she topped with fringed valances, or tailoring the fabric into upholstery and slipcovers for some of the furniture. For the guest bedroom, she chose two floral fabrics: one was used to cover a decorative bamboo folding screen, and the other—which features a lavish display of pink peonies and roses—was fashioned into a comforter cover. Combined here with the homeowners' collections of lace-trimmed bed linens, antique botanical prints, and Victorian pottery pieces, the chintzes give the room a richly romantic look.   *Continued*

The luxurious guest room above and at right, which receives abundant sunlight, has the look of a summer-

house. It is referred to as the rabbit room because of the theme of the painting and pottery.

Decorative weather vanes, such as the painted wooden peacock above, were made to sit on the rooftop of a house or barn. Although originally intended for outdoor use, antique weather vanes should be displayed indoors today to protect their painted surfaces.

As a decorator, this homeowner also has a strong interest in painted finishes and has put many of them to use—on floors, walls, and woodwork—in virtually every room of the house. Although she admits that decorative painting techniques can be time-consuming and difficult at first, she feels that the ultimate effect more than makes up for the effort.

On the floors, new finishes were applied after the wood was sanded down to its natural state. Next, parquet patterns and diamond-shaped "tiles" were sketched on, then colored with oil-

Used as a summer living room, the glassed-in porch at left houses an unusual assortment of accessories. These include a birdhouse, a heart-and-arrow weather vane, and an Indonesian carved-wood rabbit box on the floor.

base paints or stains, and sealed with a high-grade polyurethane. Many of the walls throughout the house appear to be colored a single shade, but the effect was actually created by layering two hues—such as white over pink in the sitting room and green over peach in the dining room. In this technique, the second color is dragged or combed over the first, producing a richness and depth that is impossible to achieve with a single shade. "Part of the trick," the homeowner says, "is to find colors that produce an interesting effect together. Green and peach

Continued

wouldn't seem to be compatible, but when they are put together using this method, something special happens."

While the interior is infused with color, the porches, which are used extensively for summertime living and entertaining, have a cooler, lighter look. Featuring views of the garden, one enclosed porch—bright with sunlight from wraparound windows—is filled with twig furniture, made comfortable with slipcovered cushions. "I wanted the room to have a rustic look that contrasts with the rest of the house," says the designer. "It gives me a place to put some of the primitive and folk-art pieces that we like to collect but that don't fit in well in the living room or bedrooms." Although no curtains or rugs were used on this porch, she added texture to the room by mixing kilim-covered and floral-patterned pillows on the couch and chairs. Potted plants are another element that provides a bit of color and texture, helping to link the room with the outdoors.

Indeed, the family virtually live outside during the warmer months. The lawns around the house are dotted with lovely old trees and island beds of perennials, and each spring, hundreds of narcissus bulbs bloom in profusion like wildflowers. The beauty of the gardens seems to reflect the spirit of the entire house. Nearly everything that has been done here, both inside and out, was influenced by the sense of romance that emanates from the structure itself.

The family treat their yard as an outdoor living room, enhancing it with comfortable furniture, such as the Adirondack pieces above.

*Although new, the wicker
furnishings at left recall
Victorian pieces. Arranged
on a latticed porch, they
make cool and inviting
seating on a summer
afternoon.*

COLORFUL NATURE STUDIES

While delicately rendered antique prints of flowers, birds, and other wildlife are popular decorative accessories today, most were originally intended as educational illustrations in books.

The earliest and most valuable nature studies are the botanical prints that were made from the 1600s to the early 1800s as scientific drawings. Wealthy amateur botanists, royalty, and scholarly institutions commissioned artists to record rare plants as they were introduced to Europe for cultivation. Some illustrators also traveled to exotic locales to sketch species in their native surroundings. Usually, the studies were done in watercolors, copied as engravings, printed, and hand-colored. Some of the finest botanical works of the 18th and 19th centuries were issued to subscribers in unbound sections over an extended period, to help defray printing costs. When the series was complete, subscribers often had their pages bound as books.

While early prints by known artists are costly, later 19th-century hand-colored engravings, used to illustrate popular books on nature, or volumes of poetry or essays, can still be found at reasonable prices.

The studies at left include late-18th- and early-19th-century scientific prints that were published in books, and illustrations for volumes on nature.

Santa Fe Hideaway

The furnishings in the Santa Fe living room at right were assembled one piece at a time. The tall cupboard, found at a local flea market, is filled with religious figures from Mexico. The carved wooden crucifix on the wall was also bought locally and dates from New Mexico's colonial period.

For a Dallas couple, this tiny Santa Fe adobe is the perfect holiday and summer escape, a complete departure from Texas city life. After twenty years of visiting Santa Fe, the couple bought the house out of the blue one weekend. "In retrospect, I can't imagine our lives without it," says one of the homeowners. "I've never enjoyed anything so much as working on this house and spending time here."

Built around 1840, the adobe is one of the oldest houses in Santa Fe. Its three downstairs rooms and second-floor sleeping loft look out onto a walled courtyard planted with an abundant variety of perennials that fill the yard with color all summer long.

"When we bought the house the garden was dead and the rooms were filled with stored furni-ture," one homeowner recalls. "We returned to Texas that weekend without even having taken any measurements, and I realized when I started searching for furniture that I had barely even seen the place."

Still, the age of the house, its size, and its simplicity had given the homeowners a clear impression of the kind of interior they wanted — one without anything that was new. Instead, antiques that seemed to belong in the house were collected bit by bit from around the country. In Athens, Texas, for example, the couple located three painted primitive pieces signed by their East Texas maker. An old blue chest was found during a trip to Plymouth, Massachusetts. And a long green bench, now used in the kitchen, appeared serendipitously: "My husband was

Continued

The kitchen above is color-fully decorated with family treasures both new and old. Tiny New Mexican clay pots, strung together by one of the couple's daughters, hang over the fireplace. The Windsor chairs were made in South Texas in the late 19th century, and the decorative wall cup-board is an antique piece from Mexico.

The furnishings in the bedroom above exhibit the homeowners' eclectic tastes. The pair of antique quilts was found at a Texas flea market, the lamp was created from an iron doorstop, and the green bedside table was made in East Texas.

jogging one day and saw someone heading to the Santa Fe flea market with the bench on the back of a truck. He flagged the driver down and ended up bringing the bench home."

Complementing the soft colors of Indian dhurries, braided rugs, and quilts, the cool, worn blues and greens of the furniture create a serene feeling in the house. "The colors actually remind me more of Nantucket than they do of Santa Fe," one homeowner says. "The only thing in the house that really makes use of the earthy tones usually associated with this part of the country is the painted trompe l'oeil border of Indian pots and clay figures in the living room." The border, which was painted by a local artist, was in the house when the couple

moved in. It strikes one of the homeowners as so authentic that she sometimes feels like she could reach up and take one of the pots down.

Virtually everything in the house—artwork by family friends, objects made by the couple's children, folk art, and handicrafts—has been selected, saved, and arranged with particular affection. Dedicated collectors, the homeowners spend a great deal of time in antiques shops and at shows, and are apt to bring home treasures as diverse as majolica dishes and Mexican religious objects. But they admit they have had to work at culling their collections. As much as they love finding pieces that fit in, they agree that "it would be a mistake to fill this house up too much." *Continued*

Since there were no closets in the bedroom, the owners built the one opposite out of old barn boards.

Used as a wall decoration today, this painted and gilded
cast-iron representation of
the Sacred Heart of Jesus
once adorned the door of
a Mexican convent. The
hinged front of the heart
would open to reveal a
door knocker.

In the kitchen above, the paneled cabinets, with their zigzag border, were made in the 1940s. On top of the cabinets are baskets, a majolica tureen, and a Mexican nicho, or tiny cupboard, containing figures of saints.

Indeed, what the couple enjoy most about the house is its simplicity and manageability: with room for four in the sleeping loft, the house is big enough for their children to be comfortable when they visit, yet it is small enough for them to feel cozily ensconced. "This is a wonderful place for me to work," says one owner, who is a writer and jewelry designer. "In part that's because Santa Fe has such a closely knit community of artists. Many people work at home here, and we have a great regard for one another's privacy."

Often enough, however, the courtyard garden lures this writer from her work. Both she and her husband have become avid gardeners since buying the house, and spend as much time outdoors as possible. Frequently, they eat outside at a wrought-iron table (another roadside find) that they bought along with the chairs because they liked the multicolored paint. The odd colors are typical of a house where nothing really matches. As the owners admit, "Inside and out, this house has been put together from the heart."

Enclosed by a stone and adobe wall, the courtyard garden opposite is vivid with flowers every summer. Placed just a few steps from the kitchen, the painted table and chairs are used for alfresco dining.

POTTERY OF THE ANASAZI

Evidence of a culture that has mysteriously vanished, pottery made by the Anasazi Indians is among the most intriguing crafts to emerge from the American Southwest. The beautifully decorated jugs, bowls, pitchers, and other wares are not only important as artistic expressions of this ancient people, who flourished from around A.D. 400 to 1300, but they also offer valuable clues to the nature of their lives.

The Anasazi, who were ancestors of the Pueblo Indians, settled around what is now called the Four Corners, where Utah, Arizona, New Mexico, and Colorado meet. A diverse people who spoke several different languages, they lived in communities ranging in size from a few families

Black-on-white jar, 1050-1250, Socorro

to thousands of members. Peaceable farmers, they built complex dwellings—called *pueblos* by 16th-century Spanish explorers—in the canyons, where they cultivated corn, beans, and squash.

Decorated pottery was made in several areas of the Four Corners region, and was widely traded. The names now often used to identify and categorize Anasazi wares, such as Socorro, Tularosa, and St. Johns, usually indicate the place where the pieces were made, and are associated with the regional and local styles that developed.

It is believed that the Anasazi learned about pottery from neighboring tribes around the 5th century. The pottery was made with a technique in which clay "ropes" were coiled and pinched together atop a molded base and fired over hot coals. Pieces generally have a smooth surface; the wet clay was scraped with a potshard or a piece of gourd, wood, or stone to remove modeling marks, then burnished with a pebble.

The craft was passed down through the women of the tribe, who became expert potters and raised ceramics to an art that reached its peak between 1100 and 1300. The elegant forms they

Black-on-red bowl,
1100-1300, St. Johns

Dog effigy, 850-1000, Red Mesa

created included spherical jars with high, wide necks, rounded wide-mouthed jars, or ollas, jugs with well-proportioned square shoulders, and hemispherical bowls. Many of the pieces were used for everyday household tasks, such as storing seeds and cooking the beans and corn that were the staple of the Anasazi diet.

In addition to utilitarian pottery, the Anasazi created clay effigies—naturalistic or impressionistic animals, birds, and, more rarely, human figures. While it is thought that some effigies were used in rituals, most were simply small containers such as pitchers and mugs, in animate form.

Both the utilitarian wares and the effigies are noted for their sophisticated and innovative decoration, the most distinctive aspect of Anasazi pottery. The potters preferred a

Pitcher, 725-875, Black Mesa, and jar, 1100-1250, Tularosa

white finish, although gray, brown, or red wares were made as well. Paints used to decorate the pottery were mixed with an iron-bearing mineral base (in the south and southeastern Chaco Canyon and Cibola districts) or a carbon base (in the Mesa Verde and Kayenta regions in the west and north) and were applied with fibrous yucca leaves that had been chewed to create a brushlike

tip. The finely hatched and interlocking geometric patterns—most notably, crisp black designs contrasting with a solid white background—that resulted are the hallmark of Anasazi pottery.

Many of the motifs characteristic of Anasazi pottery were adapted from those used on baskets and textiles, which the Anasazi also excelled in crafting. Decoration often consists of bands filled with geometric figures or opposing zigzags. The motifs follow the line of the ceramic form; all-over patterns seem to expand and contract depending on the shape they are following. The patterns are usually centrifugal, with repetitive designs; lines tend to demarcate the different sections of a piece—where the neck and shoulder of a jug join, for example. Pottery from the southern and southwestern regions often features stiff, angular patterns. Solid sections are combined with finely hatched areas to create a range of shadings. Pieces from the northern Kayenta region, on the other hand, are apt to display exuberant patterns that resemble weavings of the area.

By the beginning of the 14th century, the Anasazi had left their homes, perhaps driven out by invad-

Bird effigy pitcher, 1000-1115, Chaco

Bowl, 1125-1300, Tusayan or Kayenta

ers or drought. They seem to have scattered throughout the Southwest, joining other groups. But while their culture has been absorbed by that of others, their pottery survives as a fascinating record of a unique artistic achievement.

At Home
in Houston

The warmth and distinctive personality of this romantic 1940s Houston house are due in large part to its diverse furnishings, which sit together like old friends. Treasures such as tramp art and primitive paintings, garden ornaments, and hats, which the homeowner has collected over the past twenty-five years, are arranged on shelves and walls, or across mantels and tabletops.

Looking over his belongings, this collector is pleased that the kinds of objects he likes really have not changed much over time. While visits to yard sales and secondhand shops continually

Continued

Trimmed with gilded leather, the shelves of the English cupboard above contain some of the homeowner's diverse belongings, including tramp-art boxes, majolica plates, a Venetian carnival mask, a Chinese roof tile in the form of an elephant, and a mercury-glass gazing ball.

In the living room at left, a marbleized finish adds color to the mantel and crown molding.

The owner enjoys collecting pieces with an animal theme, many of which are displayed in his kitchen, above.

prompt him to enlarge his collections or even to start new ones, his old favorites always stand side by side with any new finds.

An interior designer, he is as eclectic in his choices of furniture as he is in his choices of collectibles. But, there are certain motifs that appear in both. He is particularly drawn to "faux" objects: pieces that seem to be one thing but are actually something else. For example, on his living room mantel (painted with a faux-marble finish), what looks like a stack of books topped by a lamp fixture is actually a cleverly

carved and painted wooden base with a lamp made from a chamber candlestick. Throughout the house, the owner has also found places for oddities such as Victorian maple furniture trimmed and colored to resemble bamboo, and chairs and footstools upholstered in leopard-print fabric. His interest in antique majolica was piqued initially because the pottery was often crafted and decorated to look like such organic forms as cabbage leaves, fruit, or seashells.

Most of the rooms in the house are a mix of brown, gold, and deep red tones—colors, the

Continued

The eclectic furnishings in the dining room above include a Japanese chest and a garden urn used as a vase.

Above, a rattan chair and an antique sea grass table occupy a corner of the master bedroom. A collection of hats is hung on a star-shaped Victorian hatrack, while an assortment of vintage neckties is displayed on a deer trophy.

homeowner says, that make him feel comfortable. He has combined materials with textures and patterns that enhance the ease of each room while allowing his collections to stand out. In the dining room, for instance, he used a pretty floral chintz for curtains, but paneled the walls with rough cedar boards. And in the master bedroom, brown-checked taffeta curtains are offset by walls covered with a subtle floral-print wallpaper that was designed in the late 19th century by the English artist William Morris.

Although all the rooms are old-fashioned in feeling, they do not represent any one period. Fine antiques blend comfortably with pieces that were chosen because they are merely fun. In this house every object holds a special meaning for the owner, and his eclectic possessions are the hallmark of a very personal, romantic style.

A Victorian faux-bamboo
bed, left, is the focal point of
the master bedroom. The
tiger over the bed is an
Indian shadow puppet that
the owner had framed; the
mirror is from the Black
Forest; and the pedestal
in the corner was once a
porch column on a
Houston house.

ROMANTIC TRANSFORMATIONS

Transforming an old love seat or couch with the simple addition of a pretty "slipcover" can be the first step in establishing a romantic look for a room. Indeed, with very little effort, the love seat at left became the focal point of the rooms shown here. Once covered, it also inspired the choice of related fabrics and accessories.

Above, a king-size sheet gives the love seat new life. Sheeting and other soft fabrics are ideal for creating this loosely gathered slipcover style. Simply tuck the sheet in securely under the cushions and fasten it with

pins at the outer sides. Here the addition of floral prints, antique linens, and quilts gives the room a feminine quality.

In the comfortable room above, where a tapestry bedspread is used to cover the love seat, deep colors and the contrasting patterns of an Oriental rug, a paisley shawl, and Persian-style ceramics create a more exotic variation on a romantic look. When using a heavy textile such as this bedspread, it is best simply to drape the fabric over the sofa, tucking in the seat area, rather than to try to secure it with pins.

As shown in the rooms opposite and above, a king-size sheet or a bedspread can easily be fashioned into an attractive "slipcover" for an old love seat.

THREE

Formal

*a coordinated look unified
by careful attention
to detail*

A formal interpretation of country style distinguishes the two houses presented in this chapter. The overall effect is understated. Fabrics include rich silks and chintzes rather than homespuns or gingham. Curtain treatments featuring traditional swags or valances help create a sense of elegance, as do fine antiques—inlaid mahogany tables, canopied beds, stately grandfather clocks—in the Queen Anne, Chippendale, and Federal styles.

As a rule, formal country style has a "put-together" appearance. Furnishings are coordinated, and accessories, such as delicate porcelain pieces, hunting prints, and plush pillows, are important finishing touches. Often, the look extends to architectural details as well. Many of the rooms in the two houses shown here, for example, feature delicate Georgian-period moldings, carved door pediments, and paneled overmantels. For all their elegance, however, these formal country homes do not exclude warmth. In each house, the personal touch of the owners keeps this "high" country style down to earth.

*Fine furnishings, including a mahogany-veneer Federal-style desk, strike a
formal note in a handsome master bedroom.*

Eclectic Elegance

This Maryland estate exemplifies an eclectic approach to "high-style" country design. Both inside and out, a range of elements were combined to create an elegant look for the house, which, built in stages, reflects several different architectural styles. The residence is also a testament to the tenacity and educated eye of its owners, who studied American design for years, then scoured the Middle Atlantic states and other regions for appropriate building materials and antique furnishings. The homeowners were particularly concerned with

Continued

Although the Maryland house at left looks as if it evolved over centuries, the earliest part (the small one-story wing on one end) actually dates to the 1940s. The stone "colonial" section was added in the 1970s, and the columned classical wing was built a decade later. Stone, doors, and windows salvaged from old buildings were used to achieve an aged appearance.

"doing the job right." This entailed researching period rooms at museums, as well as enlisting the aid of an architect and craftsmen who were familiar with early American building design and capable of interpreting it today.

The evolving project began years ago with the renovation and enlargement of an existing small-frame tenant house that had been built in the 1940s; its small proportions and roof trellis were inspired by those of Nantucket cottages. The central section, added in the 1970s, was modeled on the many colonial-era farmhouses in the

The 19th-century dummy board above stands at the base of a graceful staircase that came from a historic Baltimore home. The stair was restored using the old mahogany handrails and many of the two hundred original balusters.

area. The weathered walls, expertly reconstructed by masons using old tools, feature fieldstones that came from a dismantled 18th-century Pennsylvania mill. Fieldstone from the same mill was later used for the final addition, a stucco-faced library wing that contains the homeowners' six-thousand-volume reference collection on architecture, decorative arts, and gardening. With its classical portico distinguished by Ionic columns, the addition was intentionally designed to look like a "later" 19th-century extention of the main house.

Inside the residence, lustrous woods, marble flooring, classical moldings, a mix of fine antiques (including many elegant Federal-style pieces), rich fabrics, and judiciously placed

Continued

The entrance hall at left
sets the sophisticated tone
evident throughout the house.
Furnishings include a satin-
upholstered Regency sofa
and one of the few tall-case
clocks known to be the work
of John Hoff, a Pennsylvania
clockmaker of the early
1800s. The marble flooring
was rescued from a
19th-century Baltimore
town house.

Acquired in London, the
carved mantelpiece in the
living room at left was
salvaged from an 18th-
century English home. Other
period touches in this
Georgian-style room include
dentil crown molding and
silk swag draperies based
on historic designs.

accessories, such as botanicals, hunting prints, and porcelains, all contribute to the sophisticated, eclectic look. Some rooms, including the new library with its emerald sponged walls, gilt-trimmed bookcases, and glazed chintz upholstery, are quite formal. Others, like the smaller library located in an earlier section of the house, have a more relaxed character, expressed with warm wood paneling and dark country-print fabrics. And several rooms strike a balance with finely carved furniture mixed with primitive painted pieces. Says one owner, "This is a collector's house—it's very unpredictable and not typical of any one period. We want it to look as

Continued

Echoing the peach-and-green background color in the dining room are the Russian painted corner cupboard above, and the Venetian chandelier, painted Hepplewhite chairs, and floor cloth at left.

if a collector who loves everything lives here."

Among these "loves" are architectural elements such as doors, windows, moldings, paneling, flooring, stairwells, and mantelpieces that have been salvaged from old buildings awaiting demolition. For example, the small library features pine paneling from a Washington, D.C., house, a pine mantelpiece from a Maryland home, and built-in cupboards made with wallboards from a Pennsylvania log cabin.

If original period elements were unavailable or beyond repair, the couple remained undaunted. When a quantity of crown molding—preserved from a historic house once owned by an early American naval officer—chosen for the master bedroom proved to be insufficient, for example, the homeowners had new sections hand-carved to match the original. Throughout the house, grain-painted doors with badly damaged old surfaces were repainted in new colors, but with

Continued

In the small library, the pine mantel, right, is signed and dated 1812. The artwork on one wall, above,

includes 18th-century hunting prints and a shadow box made by one of the homeowners.

Located in the latest addition to the house, the new library at right features a rosewood bookcase, decorated with gilded carvings, that was designed after an English breakfront. Nine coats of glaze were used to produce the rich green finish for the walls. A witty touch is the "book" table, made of molded metal and painted to resemble a stack of old tomes.

a combed finish that was compatible with the original.

The furnishings selected for the house range from the simple to the sophisticated. While formal pieces predominate, including an inlaid mahogany dining table, a satin-upholstered Regency-style sofa, and finely carved tester beds, the owners did not rule out informal pieces such as rush-seated chairs and a well-worn Pennsylvania spice cupboard from the 1700s. Their choice of textiles reinforces this eclectic approach. Along with sumptuously draped silk swag curtains, silk and sateen bed hangings, and Oriental carpets, contemporary batik used for pillow covers, and even sheeting (made into a duvet cover), are to be found. Particularly handsome is the canvas floor cloth in the dining room, painted with a pattern the owners had admired on an expensive needlepoint rug.

Because the house contains such a mix of

Continued

The mural in the hall above, painted in twenty colors, reflects the designs of 19th-century French panoramic wallpapers and historic garden prints. To harmonize with its classical motifs, the floor was painted with a Greek key border.

The decor of the master bedroom at right was planned around the elaborate fireplace with its carved mantel, pedimented overmantel, and pictorial delft tiles. Glazed in mulberry, the tiles inspired the choice of rose tones for the carpet, the easy-chair upholstery, and the hangings on the carved walnut bed. A delicate child's chaise is placed at the foot of the bed.

Learning to stitch needle-work pictures like the one above was considered to be an important part of a proper young lady's education in the 19th century; then as now, such pieces were proudly displayed in the home. Depicting a woman and child in a garden, this antique work from England was stitched with silk thread on a linen ground.

A guest bedroom door, above, was hand-painted by one of the homeowners. The large spice cupboard is an 18th-century Pennsylvania piece.

furnishings, the couple generally favor subdued colors—soft peach, green, or blue-gray—for the background of each room. "I chose colors close to nature because they last—I never get tired of them," says one of the owners. Even the green walls in the new library and the rich tones of the adjoining hall mural were selected for their earthy feeling.

At right, folk-art pieces, such as the tramp-art box on the blanket chest and a nautical string picture made by sailors in the 1800s, furnish the guest bedroom.

Decorative Fireboards

Commonly found in America from the 1700s to the mid-1800s, fireboards offered a decorative solution to the problem of keeping fireplaces covered when they were not in use. Some fireplaces had no dampers, thereby allowing cold air and soot, as well as birds, bats, and other unwelcome visitors to descend the chimney and enter the house. Even for fireplaces with dampers, the boards were useful: they could effectively block the sight of smoke-blackened fireplace walls.

Fireboards were generally made from wood panels, battened boards, canvas stretched over a frame, or cardboard; wood was preferred because it was durable, washable, and less likely to mildew. Custom-sized to the openings they were intended to cover, the boards were designed to lean against the fireplace or were fitted with feet or molding along the bottom edge so that they could stand independently. Some featured slots cut into the bottom to accommodate a pair of andirons for support. Since the boards were intended to be ornamental as well as utilitarian, they were always decorated, frequently to coordinate with the surrounding wall surfaces. They might be covered with fabric, papier-mâché, wallpaper, stenciled designs, or freehand painting.

Painted fireboards, such as those shown here, often exhibit simple, bold compositions rendered in

Painted fireboard depicting twin girls in a paint-decorated room; oil on board with breadboard ends, eastern seaboard, 18th century

Trompe l'oeil painted fireboard of a brick fireplace with andirons, shovel, and tongs; oil on panel, Massachusetts, 1790-1800

Fireboard signed by Jonathan D. Poore, nephew of the itinerant artist
Rufus Porter; casein paint on pine board, Maine, c. 1830

Painted fireboard showing a view of Windsor, Nova Scotia, with a
trompe l'oeil frame; oil on canvas, New England, 1840-1850

strong colors. Many of the paintings were the work of itinerant limners, house painters, and other artisans, although homeowners created their own compositions as well.

Fireboard paintings covered a variety of subjects. These were often copied from popular period engravings, but they might also be inspired by people, locations, and events familiar to the owner or artist, or generated purely by the painter's imagination. Favorite themes included seascapes, landscapes, farm scenes, and historic sites. Still-life compositions, such as straw baskets brimming with fruits and vegetables, were also common. The popularity of floral arrangements for designs reflected the 18th-century English and American custom of placing sprays of greenery on an unused hearth.

Most subjects, including family portraits or a view of a town, were treated realistically; and in trompe l'oeil fireboards, realism was often combined with whimsy. One of the most common targets of these illusions was the fireplace itself: the designs faithfully reproduced brick fireplace walls, stone hearths, tiled surrounds, wooden mantels, andirons, and even a convincing film of ash on the floor. The trompe l'oeil technique was also used to simulate an elaborately carved, gilded, or grained frame around a picture; the effect was that of an oil painting resting in front of the fireplace.

A
Maryland
Manor

Nestled in the hills of Maryland's hunt country, this handsome house was resurrected from a pile of some forty-three thousand 18th-century bricks, and incorporates countless bits of architectural salvage gathered all along the eastern seaboard—every-thing from doors and dormers to tiny handmade nails. The result is both preservation project and home for a committed collector who spent four years on the undertaking, which involved re-building a 1749 house that had been previously dismantled and stored in an old barn.

Dismantled brick by brick, then moved to the site at left, this 1749 manor house was rebuilt, enlarged, and "turned" so that the original façade is now the back. The large windows allow a view of the wooded Maryland hills surrounding the house. The two telescoping additions overlook terraced gardens.

Designed for a prosperous surgeon, the original house stood by the Anacostia River, an eastern branch of the Potomac, near the tidewater territory that would become the nation's capital. Despite important historical associations—the doctor's son served in President Washington's administration and the estate was used as a hospital during the War of 1812—the house was allowed to fall into neglect over the next century. Eventually, it was slated for demolition as suburbs began to sprawl around it in the 1950s. Fortunately, a preservation-minded

Continued

The entry hall above permits a view of the den, one of the few rooms with electric lights. At night, the owner, who favors authenticity over convenience, illuminates the house primarily with candles, using such vintage holders as the mirrored "turtleback" sconces shown here.

architect took photographs and made measured drawings of the building before the structure was taken down by a local builder. Although the builder hoped to reconstruct the house elsewhere for himself, and thus carefully stored all the components, he was never able to fulfill his plan.

In the meantime, the current owner had acquired a rural wooded tract in Maryland north of Baltimore and wanted to build a colonial-style house there. Through the state preservation society, he was put in touch with the architect who had made the records of the building, and who was eager to restore the house. "He was just waiting for someone historically minded like me to come along," says the owner, recalling their first meeting. In 1961, the disassembled house

was purchased from the builder and moved to the Maryland site, and the project of rebuilding and enlarging it began.

Equipped with his own records and those found at the Historic American Buildings Survey at the Library of Congress, the architect had a ready-made plan for reconstruction. Instead of replicating the old house, however, his client chose to adapt it for modern living while faithfully retaining appropriate 18th-century details.

The initial decision was to enlarge the building. The original three-story structure with two end chimneys was consequently extended with two "telescoping" additions to accommodate a kitchen, porch, and garage. To blend in unobtrusively, the new wings were designed with

Continued

While most of the furnishings in the house are from the Queen Anne period, an exception was made for the Chippendale lowboy at left. Crafted in Philadelphia in the mid-1700s, the piece features a carved skirt, knees, and trifid feet. Walnut newel posts and balusters distinguish the closed-string staircase.

Indulging his predilection for Queen Anne furniture, the homeowner appointed the elegant drawing room at right with a number of pieces in that style, including two commode chairs with graceful serpentine rails and a walnut tea table with a scalloped skirt. The scroll-arm Queen Anne camelback sofa, one of the few reproductions in the house, is so well crafted that it has often fooled antiques experts.

Suitable accoutrements for a historic house, the 18th-century wrought-iron smokers' tools above include tongs, used to pick embers from the fire for lighting a pipe, and a fish-shaped tobacco-leaf grater.

English Liverpool ware, a type of black-printed cream-ware named after its city of origin, was primarily made from the 1760s through the early 1800s specifically to appeal to American buyers. The pitcher above is a typical piece: its design memorializes the death in 1799 of a revered national figure—George Washington.

the same jerkin-head roof line, dormers, and trim details that characterized the original building. Even the hand-molded bricks are the same as those used in the old section: since the original eighteen-inch-thick solid-brick walls of the old house were rebuilt of concrete block with a facing only a single brick deep, more than enough bricks were left over for use in the additions. As was typical of the masonry in 18th-century tidewater houses, the bricks were pointed with a mortar mixture containing crushed oyster shells.

The same attention to detail marks the interior. All of the doors, hardware, mantels, floors, paneling, moldings, glass, built-in cupboards, and other architectural elements either came from the original house or were adopted from other period buildings that had suffered a similar fate. "In the 1960s," says the owner, "people were less aware of preservation, and many old houses were demolished to make way for progress. So there was much more salvage available for the taking then than there is today."

The limited modern amenities have been kept

Continued

The dining room at left is distinguished by a cater-corner fireplace saved from the original house and a built-in corner cupboard that came from another 18th-century residence on Maryland's eastern shore. The collection of circa 1780 English creamware in the cupboard commemorates Prince William of Orange and was decorated for the Dutch market.

as unobtrusive as possible. No radiators or electric lamps are visible; instead, radiant-heat pipes are concealed under the floors, and candles provide most of the artificial light. "I did it the pure way," asserts the homeowner. Indeed, there are only three rooms with enough electric light for reading: one of the bedrooms, the den, and the kitchen. These all have small, recessed ceiling spotlights. "After all, in earlier centuries you weren't supposed to be able to read in a drawing room," he explains. "You were supposed to make polite conversation." The kitchen appliances are also carefully camouflaged. Built into the brick fireplace wall, an electric oven, for instance, is concealed behind an old iron door.

As the building progressed, the owner began hunting for suitable period furnishings and always reserved time on frequent business trips for shopping in antiques stores. The son of an avid collector, he developed an eye for quality American antiques at an early age. "I still apply the same principle today that I learned then—always buy the best you can afford." He occasionally found himself competing for a piece with Henry Francis du Pont, who was collecting for his Winterthur Museum in Delaware, and his hundred-piece service of rare 18th-century English creamware commemorating Prince William of Orange is the envy of many museum curators.

Among the more than a thousand furnishings

Continued

Bricks remaining from the original 1700s house were used for the kitchen fireplace and floor, above. The portrait of a Hereford bull adds a touch of whimsy and honors the homesite's past: some of the first species of this breed imported to America in the 1800s were raised on the acreage where the house now stands.

While most of the house conforms to a more formal appearance, the kitchen eating area opposite has a relaxed air. Although it is in the "new" wing, an 18th-century look was achieved with beams salvaged from an old Connecticut house and period furniture such as a gate-leg table and Windsor chairs.

acquired are many Queen Anne pieces, including a number of vase-splat chairs, tea tables, and drop-leaf tables, all with the curving cabriole legs characteristic of the style. Many are of walnut, a primary wood used for furniture of the early 1700s and one that the owner prefers for its rich patina. More rustic period pieces, such as the 18th-century Pennsylvania walnut dresser and painted bent-arm Windsor chairs in the breakfast room, are also to be found in the house. And, of course, necessary for a home with limited electric lighting, there are a wealth of candleholders in every room—from an Irish cut-crystal chandelier to wrought-iron candlestands.

The carved maple Sheraton field bed in the guest room at right is a family heirloom, as is the Drunkard's Path quilt, which was probably made in Virginia around 1860. At one side of the room is the two-foot-wide fireplace above, the smallest of the eleven working fireplaces in the house.

AFTERNOON TEA

Around four o'clock on most afternoons in 19th-century England, Anna, seventh Duchess of Bedford, would find herself in need of a bit of sustenance between meals. She began to request that a tray of tea, bread and sweet butter, and cakes be delivered to her bedroom. Her habit soon became known to the ladies of her acquaintance, and "afternoon tea" was born. By the end of the century, the custom of entertaining friends at afternoon tea had evolved into an elegant occasion: tea, hot dishes, and elaborate sweets were served—sometimes by footmen— and the female guests dressed in long, fancy "tea gowns."

By the mid-1800s, afternoon tea had also become fashionable in America. While the tea parties given by the American hostess may not have been as formal as those of her British counterpart, they were nevertheless important social gatherings, and lively gossip was one of the major ingredients.

The suggested behavior for both hostess and guest at an afternoon tea was prescribed by domestic writers of the day in American household manuals, etiquette books, and cookbooks. According to the 1894 volume *Etiquette,* by Agnes Morton, women were to "meet informally, chatting for a while over a sociable cup of tea, each group giving place to others, none crowding, all at ease, every one the recipient of a gracious welcome from the hostess." It was suggested that guests stay no longer than forty-five minutes (although teas actually lasted about two hours). Another author stipulated that tea, and coffee, which might also be served, were to be "drunk noiselessly, not sucked from the side of the cup, leaving the spoon in the saucer and the cup held by the handle."

An elegant tea service was as important to a successful afternoon tea as proper decorum. Most 19th-century sets were composed of a teapot, coffeepot, and hot water pot, a sugar bowl, and a cream pitcher, as well as a bowl into which cold tea could be emptied before the cup was refilled.

The table set for afternoon tea, right, reflects a fashionable 19th-century custom that has regained popularity. Among the traditional accoutrements shown here are a silver-plated tea service, a tea caddy used to store and preserve tea, a mixing glass for blending, and a strainer. Delicate cakes, sandwiches, and biscuits are customary fare.

FOUR

Casual

*setting an informal tone
with an imaginative mix
of furnishings*

🍃

At the heart of the casual country look is an easy, eclectic approach to decorating that offers plenty of opportunity for personal expression. The owners of the three houses shown in this chapter had no precise ideas of how all their furnishings would fit together; instead, they followed their own instincts and interests, picking up pieces at flea markets or refurbishing yard-sale finds, and adding all manner of accessories. As a result, these houses are refreshingly different, and clearly reflect the good time their owners had in decorating them.

In general, furnishings in a casual country home are cheerful and informal. Wicker is well suited to this relaxed look, as are basic upholstered pieces. Printed fabrics are simple—checks, plaids, stripes, and small prints—and often layered for interest. And, there is plenty of room for an innovative touch—a display of Mexican sombreros, perhaps, or a quilt folded over a pillow instead of at the foot of the bed.

*A quilt draped casually between two pine cupboards is an unexpected touch
in this country dining room.*

A Cozy Cottage

O verlooking a small pond and surround-
ed by lawns, woods, and gardens, this
charming cottage in Connecticut was
built in the 1920s for use as a child's playhouse
on a large estate. "There are people in the community who can recall being in this house as

children," the present owner says. "They all remember playing on a swing that was suspended
from a ceiling beam."

Although measuring no more than twenty feet
by twenty feet, the playhouse was sturdily built,
with heavy wood posts and beams, fieldstone

*An imaginative mix of antiques and treasures fills the living room of this Connecticut house. Yellowware
bowls keep company with brown-glazed jugs, left, while an 18th-century English chair is paired
with an American country Sheraton desk, above.*

The lusterware tea service on the top shelf in the stairwell above is a family heirloom, as is the miniature dresser.

walls, and a slate floor. When the estate was divided and sold in the 1950s, the playhouse was converted into a year-round home: the original structure remained as the living room, but a kitchen and dining area were added to the ground floor, and a second story was built in order to provide space for several bedrooms.

"The house has always reminded me of an English cottage," says the current owner, who is herself English. "I used to drive by it and admire the way it looked out over the little pond, and the way wisteria bloomed around the windows.

But it never occurred to me that I might actually live here, until the house came up for sale."

The interior of the cottage still had a dated, 1950s look—complete with knotty-pine paneling—when the owner moved in. But once she painted the paneling and remodeled the kitchen and bathrooms, the rooms began to take on the casual country look she had in mind.

A long-time devotee of auctions and tag sales, the owner has gathered furnishings and accessories that suit the unpretentious interior of the cottage. While she has always been interested in

Continued

The sampler over the mantel above came from a Welsh farmhouse, and the deer's skull from the Connecticut woods.

American and English antiques, she also seeks out pieces made by contemporary craftsmen. In addition, she likes to display "treasures"—such as abandoned birds' nests—that she discovers outdoors. Instead of following any particular home decorating plan, the owner has let the de-

cor of the house evolve simply by choosing whatever pleases her eye.

In many rooms, an unusual mix of collections sets the whimsical tone. For instance, antique yellowware bowls are placed alongside contemporary game boards, while English china is

Continued

In the kitchen, pewter pieces both antique and new are displayed in an English plate rack, above. The
homeowner made the ten-foot-long table at right from an antique base and an old floorboard.

combined successfully with a collection of pewter. And throughout the house, tables, mantels, shelves, and cupboards offer intriguing displays of imaginative finds, from hat molds and tin hatboxes to miniature furniture.

The homeowner particularly enjoys making pieces of furniture by assembling various salvaged parts. After purchasing a ten-foot-long painted table base, for example, she searched flea markets for months before locating the perfect top for it: an antique two-foot-wide floorboard, which she scraped and sanded clean. And in the master bedroom, a Federal-style tallpost bed was paired with an arched tester frame that she had bought and saved until just the right bed was found to go with it. The knotted-

Continued

The painting of an unidentified woman in the upstairs hall above was an auction find, but it resembles
a portrait of the homeowner's great-grandmother in the bedroom at right.

At right, simple swag
draperies in the guest room
allow for maximum light.
The fringed bedspreads,
which blend naturally with
the American beds and
chair, were made
in India.

and-fringed canopy, a new piece, was tea-dyed for a soft, well-used look in keeping with the old-fashioned feeling of the rest of the room.

Creative fabric treatments play a role in the decor of other rooms of the house as well. In a guest room, for example, the homeowner uses pieced quilts to cover the pillows at the heads of the twin beds, instead of folding them up at the feet, while the pretty gray-and-red backing fabric of another antique quilt becomes a kind of impromptu table cover. Such one-of-a-kind details not only reflect her imagination, but add personality to each room of the cottage, giving the home its fresh appeal.

Above, old and new treasures are placed side by side in a corner of the guest room. Although the sampler standing on the cupboard is a contemporary piece, the one hanging next to it is dated 1906.

HOME IS WHAT YOU MAKE IT

SLUMBERTIME FLOORS
that mirror the moonlight's magic

HOME IS WHAT YOU MAKE IT

Good Paint makes it a home to be proud of

WILLIAM WILLER, Sole Manufacture
CEDAR STS. MILWAUKEE WIS.

THE CAUSE OF THEIR FIRST QUARREL.
"Didn't I tell you to get Carr's **STAMPED** *Quality Ladder Tapes? Instead of which you get these wretched things, and"* — (gives way to despair).

Ever since the first books on home decoration appeared in the mid-19th century, American women have been bombarded with articles, advertisements, and practical advice. Written to appeal to the housewife on a budget, do-it-yourself decorating books have traditionally outlined ways to get the best value out of one's housekeeping dollar, and have offered suggestions on taste, quality, and timeless design. However, agreement on what constitutes timeless-ness has never lasted for very long.

In their book, *The American Woman's Home,* published in 1869, Catharine Beecher and Harriet Beecher Stowe detailed their economical approach to decorating a parlor with homemade curtains and slipcovers. "It will be a very pretty thing, now, to cut out of the same material as your lounge, sets of lambrequins, a kind of pendent curtain-top . . . to put over the windows . . . ." It was further suggested that the lambrequins be trimmed with fringe, and a tassel hung at center top.

But in 1889, in her book called *House and Home,* Marion Harland had other thoughts. "Our housewife," she said, "just hates the lambrequins overhanging the Holland shades, one large scollop in the middle, a small scollop on each side, a tassel dependent from the plumb center of the middle and biggest bulge. In sheer desperation she is sometimes tempted to throw the

THE WORK OF L.&.J.G.STICKLEY

A large portion of the better American
furnished with good furniture in plan
of L. & J. G. Stickley is the most logic
uty and a maximum of

STICKLEY, FAY

WINDOW HANGINGS

A WINDOW TREATMENT THAT LOOKS PARTICULARLY WELL IN A DINING ROOM WITH PANELED WALLS

AN ATTRACTIVE SUGGESTION FOR A TWO-PART BEDROOM WINDOW

In the homes of America where good taste rules in the furnishings, Blabon Art Floors of Linoleum are finding increasing
favor. Artistic patterns and beautiful color harmonies adapt them
for every room in the house. Inlaid pattern 164 is shown
here. Ask your dealer or write us for illustrated booklet.

THE GEORGE W. BLABON COMPANY, PHILADELPHIA

BLABON ART Linoleums

HAPPY REUNION.
They bought Carr's STAMPED Quality Ladder Tapes, and lived happy ever afterwards.

LOUIS H. MESENBRINK,
FURNITURE
922 MILWAUKEE AVENUE,
CHICAGO, ILL.

dozen chairs frantically at the piano that has stood in the same place for seventeen years."

In 1910, however, Virginia Van De Water was firm on the subject of holding onto those old chairs. "Fortunately, some of the old things are the most artistic. All of us love the old mahogany pieces, the huge arm-chairs with the 'wings' at the sides, the work stands with the 'leaves' on each end," she said in *From Kitchen to Garret*. And by 1916, decorator

Ekin Wallick was telling readers of his book, *The Attractive Home,* how to coordinate their antiques or "old mahogany pieces" with color. "If, for instance, the house is Colonial in design and the woodwork through-out is white, this fact alone sug-gests mahogany furniture," Wallick pointed out. But he warned, "The combination of oak furniture and white woodwork is seldom harmo-nious . . . ."

In 1925 the *Modern Priscilla Home*

Furnishing Book agreed, suggesting that "Color schemes, in reality, are a great deal like music. The dominant chords cannot stand alone without other notes, or the whole would not be music." But *Modern Priscilla* also offered the following practical advice to young housewives: "Do be sensi-ble about color. Even if you 'just adore pink' remember that a living-room is larger than a bridal bouquet and the color scheme is to last longer than a pink tea."

New Mexico Farmhouse

Situated in a small valley just outside of Santa Fe, this Victorian-style farmhouse recalls the vernacular architecture common in northern New Mexico in the 1880s. Although often mistaken for a restoration, the house is new, designed and built by the homeowners themselves.

The house gains its character from its many traditional details. In one corner of the living room, for instance, is a shepherd's fireplace: its

Continued

Tall, multipaned windows allow plenty of light into the plant-filled sunroom above. The chair is a type once used by barbers in Mexico.

Regional furnishings in the living room at left include a rare 1930s Santa Fe stool.

Among the regional crafts in the dining room above is an unusual checkered rag rug made by a weaver from northern New Mexico.

flat top was originally designed to provide sheepherders in mountain huts with a warm place to sleep at night. Textured ceilings also add to the regional look. In this room, a coved ceiling is formed from arched plaster sections divided by *vigas*, or log beams. In contrast to this meticulous plasterwork, the ceilings in the kitchen and dining room are made from rough split-cedar boards that are arranged in herringbone fashion between the *vigas*. The cedar imparts a light, fresh scent to these rooms.

Other details that add authenticity include the interior doors of the house, custom-made by local craftsmen who model their designs on

Continued

In the kitchen opposite, an antique traveling salesman's rack holds spices. Contemporary tin figures, called "farmwives on their way to heaven" by their local maker, form an unusual wall display. The gingerbread-trimmed window opens onto the dining room.

The pine post in the guest bedroom at right is nearly twenty-four feet long, extending from the peak of the roof down to the first floor. It makes a convenient display place for a collection of sombreros.

fragments of early New Mexican woodwork. The antique leaded-glass windows, particularly prized by the homeowners, were found at local salvage companies and flea markets.

Furnishings throughout the house are a lighthearted mix of Victorian antiques, family heirlooms, and regional pieces. Most of the hand-crafted furniture, woven rugs, and artwork—both antique and contemporary—used in the downstairs rooms comes from Mexico and northern New Mexico. Many of the whimsical pieces, such as the carved wooden animal figures

and colorful pottery tableware collected by the homeowners, are the work of local craftspeople who are friends of the family. One of the homeowners also collects child-size chairs; one chair, in an upstairs guest bedroom built under a steeply pitched roof, is a rare small form of a type of furniture made in Santa Fe in the 1930s.

Other traditional southwestern furnishings, as well as 19th-century pieces from one owner's family home in Michigan, enhance the casual, eclectic feeling in this bedroom. And accessories such as Navajo rugs from the 1930s and

Continued

The upper panel on every door in the house has a different design. The double doors above were copied from a pair in a New Mexico church.

Printed advertisements, in the form of package labels, posters, and trade cards such as those above, became an art form in the mid-19th century. Today they are collected for their lively slogans and amusing pictures.

1940s and a collection of Mexican sombreros are natural additions to the decor.

The bathrooms, also distinctive, are finished with Mexican tiles, which provide a colorful backdrop for a display of some unusual antiques. The sink cabinet in the upstairs bath, for example, was adapted from an old dry sink with a galvanized tin top, which was made by a Mennonite sect in Mexico: the homeowners installed the sink basin and brass-and-porcelain taps. They also attached antique glass-shaded

lamps to a Victorian looking-glass above the sink, and found an old brass shower curtain rod that suited the claw-footed tub. The downstairs bathroom is fitted with a vintage washstand, and a scroll-edged shelf with pegs, for towels.

Fending off the instinct to have it all done at once, the owners have put together these eclectic furnishings gradually so that they could achieve just the right blend of old and new. The pleasing result is a comfortable home flavored with regional accents.

A free-standing tub gives an old-fashioned look to the upstairs bathroom, above. Unusual accessories in the downstairs bath, opposite, include a large, contemporary hand-carved fish displayed on a shelf, and a picture frame that, without a picture, becomes a decoration in its own right.

Phase One blanket, c. 1800-1850

Phase Two blanket, c. 1860-1870

Phase Two blanket, c. 1865-1870

Phase Two blanket, c. 1870-1875

Phase Three blanket, c. 1870-1875

Phase Three blanket, c. 1880-1890

Navajo Chief Blankets

Richly colored and superbly woven, chief blankets are a distinctive type of woolen textile made by the Navajo from about 1800 to the 1890s. The term is actually a misnomer because there were no "chiefs" in the Navajo community, and the blankets could be used by any member of the tribe. These textiles were highly valued, however, and ownership conferred an aura of achievement and prestige. Most were produced for trade, and were widely sought after by members of many different tribes, from the Southwest to the Great Plains, including the Sioux, Ute, and Blackfoot.

Intended to be worn over the shoulders, chief blankets are always wider than they are long, with patterns designed to drape and move gracefully. The striped patterns run horizontally, with the broad central band meant to suggest a belt. On more elaborate examples, motifs are positioned at the center and edges of the blankets, so that they fall at the back and front of the wearer; the partial patterns on the ends are intended to meet when the blanket is wrapped around the body.

These distinctive blankets, woven exclusively by women, are generally classified in three styles, or phases, which correspond to developments in the patterns and to related changes in the materials used. The dates for each phase are approximate, as styles overlapped. Phase One blankets (1800-1850) feature the simplest designs—bands in varying widths and colors—and were made primarily with yarns that the Navajo spun from the long, straight fleece of the churro sheep they raised.

Blankets from Phase Two (1850-1875) display more complex pat-

Watercolor portrait of a Piegan Blackfoot Indian wearing a Phase One chief blanket; Karl Bodmer, 1833

terns. The bands are interrupted by stripes, squares, blocks, zigzags, and other geometric shapes. A taste for bolder colors was reflected in the use of a crimson baize cloth from England. The cloth—called *bayeta* by the Spanish, who introduced it to the Southwest—was in great demand among the Navajo because they were unable to obtain fabric in such a bright color from local sources. The weavers laboriously raveled the cloth, plied the strands to the desired thickness, and incorporated them into their blankets. Another commercially made material adopted during this phase was saxony yarn, a fine, naturally dyed type originally from Europe.

In Phase Three (1860-1900), the blanket designs became more dramatic and sophisticated. The twelve-block pattern was reduced to a nine-block pattern, while the controlled angular motifs evolved into jagged-edge diamonds that seem to explode against the striped field. In this period, the Navajo also came to rely more on new, often inferior materials. Instead of high-quality *bayeta*, the Indians raveled American wool flannels, which yielded short, fuzzy threads. In 1864, coarse Germantown yarns, made near Philadelphia, began replacing the silky saxony yarns. Both the cloths and the yarns were colored with chemical dyes, which, although they were more vivid, faded more readily than natural dyes.

After the 1890s, few chief blankets were produced. The Navajo no longer had the materials to create high-quality textiles, and their primary market—other Native Americans—had dwindled as various tribes were wiped out or were sent to reservations. Eventually, the Navajo turned their looms to rugs, increasingly in demand by a non-Indian market.

California Casual

The turn-of-the-century wicker sofa above is from the owner's family home in Michigan. The contemporary folk-art dogs on the tabletop here and at right were chosen in homage to her pets.

The owner of this northern California house was delighted when she found the property: it offered privacy, splendid views of the ocean, and plenty of space for her dogs to romp freely. But the house itself, a modern stucco residence built in the 1950s, was not what she had in mind as a year-round country home. So, with the help of an architect, she set out to redesign the house inside and out.

The primary design objective was that the renovated residence have the unaffected warmth and charm of an old cottage. To that end, a subdued beige-and-white color scheme and simple

Continued

Victorian pine pieces, a softly colored Oriental rug, and an abundance of overstuffed pillows impart a casual elegance to this California living room.

country furniture, including wicker and pine pieces, are used throughout.

"Aged" architectural elements also play a role in the decor. For instance, the ceiling beams and boards in the living room were originally left outdoors to weather and crack slightly before they were put in place. Once installed, the beams were given a light wash of white paint to accentuate their worn appearance. And in the kitchen, cupboards with punched-aluminum doors and simple chrome pulls were designed to complement the old-fashioned beaded-board paneling on the walls.

Even the choice of smaller details, such as the light fixtures, received careful thought. Tin-shaded lamps found at an Army-Navy store, for

Continued

Flea-market finds were put to creative use throughout the house. In the kitchen at left, a glass vase
from an old touring car was installed above the sink. And for the dining room above, a tabletop
was created from two antique doors.

A woven rag rug gives a
homey look to the guest room
at right. The leaded-glass
lamp, wrought-iron bed,
quilt, and antique linens are
all family heirlooms.

Multipaned windows in a variety of sizes were used in remodeling the house, so that the exterior would not have a uniform appearance. In the bathroom at right, window installation had to wait until the old-fashioned tank toilet was found and put in place.

example, were perfect for providing simple, overhead lighting. Other imaginative fixtures that enhance the old-fashioned look include the antique leaded-glass lamps that are found throughout the house, and a porcelain-and-brass chandelier. All of these are heirlooms that the owner brought to California from her family home in Michigan.

It is just this mix of family pieces and salvaged finds that produces the cozy, easy feeling that characterizes the house. Filled with comfortable furniture and favorite handcrafts, as well as flowers picked from the garden, the cottage is casual and comfortable, always a welcoming place to come home to.

The Victorian oak washstand above—appointed with antique hand towels, a bowl of scented soaps, and an ironstone washbasin and pitcher—gives the bathroom the fresh, simple look of an earlier era.

FIVE

Projects
for the Home

*let your imagination
be your guide*

🍃

One of the greatest pleasures in decorating comes from putting your own hands to work. A hand-crafted project will not only let you express your tastes in color and design, but will also reward you with the satisfaction of creating something that is like no other.

This chapter includes directions for four original projects: making a fabric-covered memento board, trimming a shelf unit, combing a door, and stenciling a floor border with wood stain. The effects are quite striking and the projects, for the most part, are actually simple to do; only the stenciled floor border requires some previous craft experience. The photographs of each finished project are meant only as inspiration. For example, the memento board on page 162 is shown with a damask covering, but a handsome flannel or an elegant silk might be equally effective. Similarly, the shelf unit on page 165 could be trimmed with any style of decorative molding. In all cases, the color choices are completely up to you.

*Graining combs and decorative molding are among the materials needed for the projects
in this chapter. Experiment with colors and patterns before you begin.*

CRAFTING A MEMENTO BOARD

Y ou can turn a plain cork bulletin board into an elegant organizer and showcase for family photographs and other mementos with the simple addition of paint, pretty fabric, and ribbon. You may use any size board (the board shown here measures 16 x 24 inches), but make sure that the frame is removable; it will be taken off, spatter-painted, then reattached after the corkboard is covered, concealing the raw edges of the fabric and ribbons. You will need to experiment with the width of the ribbons, which are laid down in an intersecting pattern of parallel diagonals, and with the distance between them, to suit the size of your board.

A. After the frame is painted with a light base color, it is spattered with darker paint flicked from a toothbrush.

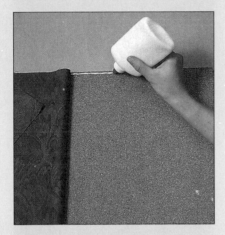

B. To attach the fabric to the cork bulletin board, white glue is applied ⅛ inch in along each edge.

C. Working out from the center of the board, attach ribbons on the diagonal at even intervals.

MATERIALS

· Cork bulletin board, ½ inch thick, with removable frame ·
· Cotton or other sturdy fabric to cover board ·
· Ribbon (grosgrain, satin, or velvet recommended) ·
· Acrylic paint in two colors, one light and one dark ·
· Decorative upholstery tacks ·
· Toothbrush · 1-inch paintbrush ·
· White glue · Measuring tape · Ruler ·
· Tailors' chalk · Scissors ·
· Newspaper ·

◆

DIRECTIONS

1. Remove the frame from the bulletin board and set the board and hardware aside.

2. Place the frame on a flat work surface. Using the paintbrush, apply one coat of the light-colored acrylic paint to the frame and let dry.

3. Using the toothbrush and the dark acrylic paint, practice your spattering technique on some newspaper. Dip the toothbrush into the paint so that it is wet but not dripping. Holding the toothbrush about 1 inch above the paper with the bristles down, lightly run your thumb over the bristles. Once you have learned how to get the spatter density you like, use the technique to spatter-paint the frame (Illustration A). Let dry.

4. Press the fabric. With the right side down, lay the fabric on the work surface. Place the bulletin board on the fabric; if the fabric is patterned, adjust it until you like the way the pattern falls. Trace the board. Cut out the fabric and press again.

5. To attach the fabric to the board, run a line of glue ⅛ inch in along one edge; lay the fabric on top and press down as you go (Illustration B). In the same manner, glue the fabric to the adjacent edges of the board, gently pressing out any wrinkles. Glue the remaining edge.

6. Measure the diagonal distance between two corners of the board and cut two pieces of ribbon to this length.

7. Measure to find the exact center of the board and mark it. Cross the pieces of ribbon and secure them with an upholstery tack where they intersect at the marked center of the board. Stretch the ribbons out taut to meet the corners of the board, and glue at each edge.

8. Determine the distance you want between parallel ribbons. Measure that distance down from the bottom edge of one of the two intersecting ribbons and, using the tailors' chalk and the ruler, mark a diagonal line from one edge of the board to the other. Lay the top edge of the remaining ribbon on this line and stretch on the diagonal to the edges of the board (Illustration C); cut a piece of ribbon to this length and glue in place at the board edges.

9. In the same manner, mark lines, cut pieces of ribbon, and glue the ribbons at equal intervals until the board is covered. Place a tack at each intersection.

10. Reattach the painted frame to the bulletin board using the original hardware.

TRIMMING A SHELF

To give plain shelving a custom-made look, paint it in imaginative color combinations and then add decorative molding for dimension and interest. You can refurbish an old unit, or start with new, unfinished shelving, available at home improvement stores. Molding strips can also be purchased there, as well as at lumber yards or hardware stores.

The shelf unit shown here measures 20 x 30 inches, but you can use any size unit you want. If your molding has a repeating design, be sure to position the strip on the shelf and mark it before cutting it to size, adjusting it so that the pattern breaks where it looks the best.

A. A miter box can be used to ensure that the ends of the molding pieces are cut at a 90-degree angle.

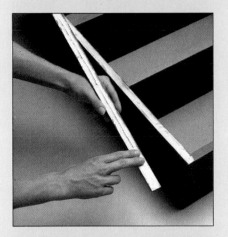

B. For a firmer hold, the glue is spread out evenly with the fingers on both the shelf unit and the molding.

C. A nail set makes it easy to sink the wire brads below the surface of the molding.

MATERIALS

· Shelf unit ·

· Molding strips in designs desired, to fit shelf unit edges ·

· Latex primer · Semigloss latex paint in colors desired ·

· 2-inch paintbrush · 1-inch paintbrush · Artists' paintbrush ·

· 1 small can wood putty (optional) ·

· Hammer · ¾-inch wire brads · ¹⁄₃₂-inch nail set ·

· Coping saw · Miter box (optional) ·

· Fine sandpaper · Tack cloth ·

· White glue ·

◆

DIRECTIONS

1. Sand the shelf unit and wipe clean with the tack cloth. Using the 2-inch brush, apply one coat of primer and let dry.

2. Using the 1-inch brush, apply paint to the shelf unit in the colors desired; let dry thoroughly and repeat with a second coat.

3. Measure the length of one side of the front of the shelf unit and, using the coping saw (and the miter box if you have one), cut a piece of molding to that measurement (Illustration A); before cutting be sure that the pattern on the molding falls the way you want it to at the ends. Repeat for the opposite side and for the top and bottom of the shelf, making sure to subtract the width of the side molding pieces when measuring for the top and bottom pieces. Sand the cut ends of the molding pieces. Cut additional molding for the fronts of the shelves if desired.

4. Using the artists' brush, paint the molding pieces in the colors desired; let dry thoroughly and repeat with a second coat.

5. Run a line of glue along the front of one side of the shelf unit and smooth out with your fingers; apply glue to the back of the corresponding molding piece in the same manner (Illustration B). Press the molding to the front of the shelf unit. Immediately hammer in brads at even intervals for reinforcement, using the nail set to sink them (Illustration C). Repeat for the opposite side and the remaining top, bottom, and shelf molding pieces.

6. Fill in the nail holes with wood putty; sand if desired. Touch up with paint if necessary.

COMBING A DOOR

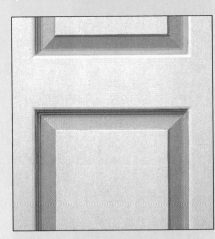

A. Before glazing, the door is painted with one or two (or more) base colors as desired.

B. After all the stiles of the door are decorated, the rails are combed so that the patterns meet at the junctures.

C. The panels of the door are combed last. Here a brown glaze contrasts effectively with a green glaze.

Combing is a decorative painting method that involves applying a tinted glaze over a base color, then running a comb through the glaze to create a pattern. You can experiment with zigzag or wavy designs to get any look you like, but because the technique can be tricky, it is a good idea to practice before beginning your project.

Combing is a good choice for a paneled door, where colors and patterns can be effectively contrasted in the different sections. Using a light, bright color for the base coat and a darker glaze maximizes the effect. You can choose two or three base-coat colors and vary the glaze colors. The door shown here has a cream-colored base coat, and the beveled panels are edged in yellow; the glazing is in green and brown tints.

Powdered pigments and graining combs are available at fine art-supply and crafts stores. Avoid blue pigment—it does not comb smoothly.

MATERIALS

· 1 quart latex primer ·
· 1 quart semigloss latex paint in each base color desired ·
· Powdered pigments in colors desired, for glazing ·
· Light corn syrup · White vinegar · 1 quart satin-finish polyurethane ·
· Various graining or other combs, from 1 to 3 inches ·
· 4-inch paintbrush · 1-inch paintbrush · Artists' paintbrush ·
· Medium-fine sandpaper · Paper towels ·

◆

DIRECTIONS

1. Using the 4-inch brush, prime the door and let dry. Sand lightly.

2. Apply the desired base-paint colors (Illustration A); let dry 24 hours.

3. To make the glaze, place ½ teaspoon corn syrup in a small container. Add 1 teaspoon pigment and blend well, using the artists' brush, until the mixture forms a paste. Mix in 2 tablespoons vinegar and blend well. (This small amount of glaze is enough to cover the door.)

4. Glaze and comb all the vertical members, or stiles, of the door first, working one section at a time. Using the 1-inch brush, apply the glaze to part of one stile, working the glaze back and forth and up and down until it is smooth and free of bubbles. If the glaze does not seem dark enough, apply additional coats before combing. When the color is satisfactory, comb while the glaze is still wet, using any combination of combs you like. (If you don't like the pattern, simply wipe it off with a paper towel dampened with vinegar, and start over.) Continue glazing and combing until the entire stile is finished.

5. After all the stiles are decorated, comb the horizontal sections, or rails, blending the patterns well at the junctures (Illustration B).

6. Comb the panels last (Illustration C); let the glaze dry thoroughly.

7. Apply two or three coats of polyurethane for protection following the manufacturer's directions.

Stenciling a floor border using wood stain is a good way to achieve the effect of more expensive wood inlay. This is not a project for a beginner, however, and even if you are an experienced stenciler, you should practice the technique on scraps of unfinished wood; if the stain seeps under the edges of the stencil, it will be difficult to remove. Spraying the stencil with adhesive before laying it down will help prevent seepage; it is also important to dab most of the stain off the brush before you begin stenciling.

You can buy ready-made stencils at crafts stores, or cut your own from clear acetate. Most precut border stencils come with a corner motif; if not, you will want to plan your pattern carefully to get the design placement you want in the corners.

The directions opposite call for wood stains in a medium and a dark color (a light stain may become invisible when polyurethane is applied).

Be sure to apply the darker stain first. Let each stenciled section dry before moving the stencil. Drying generally takes just a few minutes, but may take longer in humid weather. Letting the stain evaporate in its container a bit before applying it may make the job easier.

Since the technique will not work on a finished floor, you must either start with a newly laid floor, or sand off the existing finish on an old floor, a job best left to a professional.

A. The stencil is sprayed with adhesive on the back and taped at the edges to keep it firmly affixed to the floor.

B. Before the stain is applied, the stencil brush should be dabbed on paper towels until it is nearly dry.

C. The stencil for the second color is aligned over the first color using register marks for placement.

MATERIALS

· Geometric border stencils in design of choice ·
(preferably with corner motif)
· Wood stain in two colors, one dark and one medium ·
· Semigloss polyurethane to cover floor ·
· 2 stencil brushes ·
· White artists' tape or masking tape ·
· Spray adhesive · Ruler ·
· Paper towels ·

◆

DIRECTIONS

1. Sand the floor if necessary. Vacuum the floor clean. Tape the baseboards to protect them from any stain that might spatter.

2. Determine how far you want the border to be from the baseboards and, measuring carefully with a ruler, draw a light pencil line all the way around the floor to mark.

3. Spray the back of the stencil to be used for the darker stain with adhesive. At one corner of the room, position the stencil along the marked line and press so that it adheres to the floor. Tape the edges to secure (Illustration A).

4. Dip the end of a stencil brush into the darker stain, then dab off most of the stain onto paper towels; the brush should be almost dry. Holding the brush perpendicular to the stencil, apply the stain in an up-and-down tamping motion, working from the center of the stencil toward the edges (Illustration B). When you apply the stain, it should have a transparent appearance; it is best to apply several light coats rather than one dark coat, to ensure crisp, even edges. Allow the stain to dry between coats.

5. Repeat, repositioning the stencil and aligning the register marks, along the marked line all the way around the room.

6. Repeat the process using the second stencil and the lighter stain (Illustration C). Let the border dry thoroughly, then apply two or three coats of polyurethane to the entire floor following the manufacturer's directions.

Photography Credits

Cover, frontispiece, and pages 24-25, 26, 27, 28, 29, 30, 31, 43 (right), 54 (left), 62-63, 64 (except 64 left), 65, 66-67, 68, 69, 70, 71, 72-73 (except 72 left), 74, 75, 94, 96-97, 98, 99, 100-101, 102, 103, 104, 105, 106, 107, 108-109 (except 109 right), 110, 111, 120 (right), 128, 130, 131, 132, 133, 134, 135, 136, 137, 138, 139: George Ross. Pages 8, 10, 11, 12, 13, 14, 15, 16, 17, 18, 19, 20-21, 34, 35, 36-37, 38, 39, 40, 41, 42, 43 (except 43 right), 46, 48, 49, 50-51, 52, 53, 54 (except 54 left), 55, 56, 57, 58-59 (except 59 right), 60-61, 76-77, 78, 79, 80, 81, 82, 92, 93, 114-115, 116, 117, 118-119, 120-121 (except 120 left), 122, 123, 124, 125, 126-127, 142, 143, 144, 145, 146, 147, 148 (except 148 left, both), 149, 160, 164 (except 164 top), 165, 168, 169: Steven Mays. Page 22: Harvard Law Art Collection. Page 23 (top): from *English & Oriental Carpets at Williamsburg* by Mildred Lanier, published by the Colonial Williamsburg Foundation. Page 23 (bot-tom): Philadelphia Museum of Art, John D. McIlhenny Collection. Pages 44-45: (fan chair) Bill Holland from *The Windsor Style in America* by Charles Santore, published by Running Press, Philadelphia, PA; (candlestand and sack-back high-chair) Bill Holland from *The Windsor Style in America, Volume II* by Charles Santore, published by Running Press, Philadelphia, PA; (continuous-arm settee and bow-back armchair with applied rockers) Jon Elli-ott; (chair-table) Shelburne Museum, Shel-burne, Vermont; (footstool) courtesy of David A. Schorsch, Inc., NYC. Pages 59 (right), 64 (left): Michael Luppino. Pages 72 (left), 109 (right): Jon Elliott. Page 83: Evans Caglage. Pages 84-85: Jerry Jacka Photography. Pages 86, 87, 88, 89, 90, 91: Bill Stites. Page 112 (top): Wayne Pratt & Co., Fine American Antiques, Marlboro, MA. Pages 32-33, 112 (bottom), 113 (bottom): J. David Bohl, courtesy of the Society for the Preservation of New Eng-land Antiquities, Boston, MA. Page 113 (top): America Hurrah, NYC. Pages 140-141 (top row, left to right): Kit Barry, Brat-tleboro, VT; *Woman's Home Companion*, November, 1930, courtesy of Bonnie J. Slotnick; *Better Homes & Gardens*, June, 1939, courtesy of Bonnie J. Slotnick; The New York Public Library Picture Collec-tion; The New York Public Library Picture Collection; The New York Public Library Picture Collection; (bottom row, left to right): Kit Barry, Brattleboro, VT; *Better Homes & Gardens*, June, 1939, courtesy of Bonnie J. Slotnick; both, The Granger Collection, NYC; from *The Attractive Home* by Ekin Wallick, published by the Car-penter Morton Co., Boston, MA; Bett-mann Archive, NYC. Page 148 (left): cour-tesy of Bonnie J. Slotnick. Page 150: all photos (except top left): Natural History Museum of Los Angeles County, Los An-geles, CA; (top left): Museum of New Mex-ico, Santa Fe. Pages 152, 153, 154, 155, 156-157 158, 159: Laurie Black. Pages 162, 163, 164 (top), 166, 167: Tria Giovan.

Prop and Design Credits

The Editors would like to thank the follow-ing for their contributions as designers or consultants or for their courtesy in lending items for photography. Items not listed are privately owned. **Cover**: interior designed and decorated by Pat Rosiak of Byford & Mills, Fairhaven, NJ. **Page 8**: curtains—Sandy Riffelmacher, Westfield, NY. **Pages 10-11**: Rufus Porter School mural—Debra Darnall, Columbus, OH. **Page 13**: sofa—William Hromy Antiques, Wadsworth, OH. **Pages 16-21**: curtains—Sandy Riffel-macher, Westfield, NY. **Pages 18-21**: sten-ciled border—Debra Darnall, Columbus, OH. **Pages 22-23**: consultant—Sarah B. Sherrill. **Pages 24-31**: eighteenth-century restoration consultant—William Bake-man, Wilbraham, MA; historical research—Mark Williams, Salmon Brook Histori-cal Society, Granby, CT; restoration super-visor—Jeffrey Walker, Creative Structures, Granby, CT. **Pages 26-27**: stenciling re-created by John Canning, Kensington, CT. **Pages 32-33**: Moses Eaton, Jr., stencils and stenciled section of plaster wall courtesy of the Society for the Preservation of New England Antiquities, Boston. **Page 34**: so-fa—Nancy Kalin Designs, North Canton, OH. **Pages 34-43**: all Windsor chairs and tiger-maple harvest table—Richard Grell, The Windsor Chairmaker, Hudson, OH. **Pages 46-59**: interiors by Ron Grimaldi, NYC; all fabrics and wallcoverings—Rose Cumming, Ltd., NYC. **Page 57**: wall-covering border—Brunschwig & Fils, NYC. **Pages 60-61**: all gingerbread pieces, solid pine—Vintage Wood Works, Dept. 1136, Fredericksburg, TX, 78624; all paint colors from Heritage Colors, Collection II—The Sherwin-Williams Company, Cleve-land, OH. **Pages 64-75**: interiors designed and decorated by Pat Rosiak of Byford & Mills, Fairhaven, NJ. **Pages 76-77**: antique books—Jutta Buck, Antiquarian Book and Print Seller, NYC; antique botanical prints—Ursus Books and Prints, Ltd., NYC. **Pages 84-85**: consultant—Bill Schenck, Moran, WY. **Pages 86-91**: interiors designed by Jerry Jeanmard of Wells De-sign, Houston, TX. **Page 92**: antique Eng-lish plates on wall—Bardith, Ltd., NYC; prints on wall, (left) Currier & Ives hand-colored lithograph in folk-art frame, (right) George Brookshaw, "Pomona Britanni-ca"—Ursus Books and Prints, Ltd., NYC; sisal flooring, hand-hooked wool rug—ABC International Design Rugs, NYC; vintage floral pillows—A Touch of Ivy, NYC, also available at ABC Bed, Bath, and Linens, NYC; white lace pillow—paper white ltd., Fairfax, CA. **Page 93**: antique English plates on wall—Bardith, Ltd., NYC; "Harlequin" teacup and saucer—Thaxton & Company, NYC; sisal flooring, antique Oriental rug—ABC International Design Rugs, NYC; purple moiré pillow—ABC Bed, Bath, and Linens, NYC. **Pages 94-111**: interiors designed and decorated by Eleanor Weller of Charlotte's Webb Interiors and Associates, Monkton, MD; architectural design—Bryden Hyde, Baltimore, MD, as adapted by Frank H. Weller, Jr.; builder of stone section of house—Ed Nace, Hanover, PA. **Pages 108-109**: curtains and bed dressing—Robert Zimmerman, Baltimore Museum, Baltimore, MD; bed dressing recut by John Buckwalter, Carlyle, PA. **Pages 126-127**: silver-plate Victorian tea and cof-

fee service (c. 1845), silver-plate Victorian tea tray (c. 1860), silver-plate Victorian cake stand (c. 1870), oak and silver Victorian tea caddy (c. 1880), Continental silver tea strainer and bowl (c. 1820), carved mother-of-pearl tea caddy spoon (c. 1870), mother-of-pearl-handled cake knife—James II Galleries, Ltd., NYC; Royal Albert "Heirloom" bone china teacups and saucers, dessert plates—Royal Doulton, USA, Inc., Somerset, NJ; "Clouds" ivory tablecloth—Le Jacquard Français/Palais Royal, Charlottesville, VA; white-lace-edged napkins—Frank McIntosh at Henri Bendel, NYC. **Pages 142-149**: interiors designed and built by Clemens Construction, Santa Fe, NM. **Page 142**: painted wooden snake—Richard Davila, Santa Fe, NM; painted child's chair—Jackalope, Santa Fe, NM. **Page 144**: tableware—Mei Ming Pottery, Santa Fe, NM; ceramic guinea hen—Jenny Lind/Allen Walter, Sante Fe,

NM. **Page 145**: painted tiles behind stove—Animals and Friends, Santa Fe, NM. **Page 148**: trade cards—collection of Bonnie J. Slotnick, NYC. **Page 149**: painted wooden fish—Richard Davila, Santa Fe, NM; ceramic frog—Jenny Lind/Allen Walter, Santa Fe, NM. **Pages 152-159**: interiors designed by Jan Johnston Associates, Oakland, CA. **Page 160**: combed samples designed and executed by Rubens Teles/Jay Johnson's America's Folk Heritage Gallery, NYC. **Page 162**: wallcovering, "Crab Apple" #CAW-550—Bradbury & Bradbury Wallpapers, Benicia, CA. **Pages 162-163**: memento board executed by Ginger Hansen Shafer, NYC. **Pages 164-165**: shelf executed by Ginger Hansen Shafer, NYC. **Pages 166-167**: door decoration designed and executed by Rubens Teles/Jay Johnson's America's Folk Heritage Gallery, NYC. **Pages 168-169**: floor border designed and executed by Ginger Hansen Shafer, NYC.

Index

Acknowledgments

Our thanks to Gemma and Gene Baker, Jutta Buck, Chris Clemens, Judith and Dennis Conrad, Mr. and Mrs. Leonard Crewe, Jr., Gillian Edwards, Barbara Foss, Ronald A. Grimaldi, Jan Johnston, Lanni Loeks, DiAnne and Don Malouf, Mariann Rodee, Pat Rosiak, Bill Schenck, and Mr. and Mrs. Frank H. Weller, Jr., for their help on this book.

©1990 Time-Life Books Inc. All rights reserved

No part of this book may be reproduced in any form or by any electronic
or mechanical means, including information storage and retrieval devices
or systems, without prior written permission from the publisher
except that brief passages may be quoted for reviews.

First printing
Published simultaneously in Canada
School and library distribution by Silver Burdett Company,
Morristown, New Jersey

TIME-LIFE is a trademark of Time Incorporated U.S.A.

Production by Giga Communications, Inc.
Printed in U.S.A.

Library of Congress Cataloging-in-Publication Data

Country Style.
p. cm. — (American country)
ISBN 0-8094-6833-6 — ISBN 0-8094-6834-4 (lib. bdg.)
1. Decoration and ornament, Rustic—United States.
2. Interior decoration—United States.
I. Time-Life Books. II. Series.
NK2002.C64   1990   747.213—dc20   89-20480
CIP

American Country was created by Rebus, Inc., and published by Time-Life Books.

REBUS, INC.

Publisher: RODNEY FRIEDMAN · Editor: MARYA DALRYMPLE
Executive Editor: RACHEL D. CARLEY · Managing Editor: BRENDA SAVARD · Consulting Editor: CHARLES L. MEE, JR.
Senior Editor: SUSAN B. GOODMAN · Copy Editor: ALEXA RIPLEY BARRE
Writers: JUDITH CRESSY, ROSEMARY G. RENNICKE
Design Editors: NANCY MERNIT, CATHRYN SCHWING
Test Kitchen Director: GRACE YOUNG · Editor, The Country Letter: BONNIE J. SLOTNICK
Editorial Assistant: LEE CUTRONE · Contributing Editor: ANNE MOFFAT
Indexer: MARILYN FLAIG

Art Director: JUDITH HENRY · Associate Art Director: SARA REYNOLDS
Designers: AMY BERNIKER, TIMOTHY JEFFS
Photographer: STEVEN MAYS · Photo Editor: SUE ISRAEL
Photo Assistant: ROB WHITCOMB · Freelance Photographers: JON ELLIOTT,
TRIA GIOVAN, GEORGE ROSS
Freelance Photo Stylist: VALORIE FISHER

Series Consultants: BOB CAHN, HELAINE W. FENDELMAN, LINDA C. FRANKLIN, GLORIA GALE,
KATHLEEN EAGEN JOHNSON, JUNE SPRIGG, CLAIRE WHITCOMB

Time-Life Books Inc. is a wholly owned subsidiary of THE TIME INC. BOOK COMPANY.

President and Chief Executive Officer: KELSO F. SUTTON
President, Time Inc. Books Direct: CHRISTOPHER T. LINEN

TIME-LIFE BOOKS INC.

Editor: GEORGE CONSTABLE · Executive Editor: ELLEN PHILLIPS
Director of Design: LOUIS KLEIN · Director of Editorial Resources: PHYLLIS K. WISE
Editorial Board: RUSSELL B. ADAMS JR., DALE M. BROWN, ROBERTA CONLAN, THOMAS H. FLAHERTY,
LEE HASSIG, JIM HICKS, DONIA ANN STEELE, ROSALIND STUBENBERG
Director of Photography and Research: JOHN CONRAD WEISER

President: JOHN M. FAHEY JR.
Senior Vice Presidents: ROBERT M. DeSENA, JAMES L. MERCER, PAUL R. STEWART,
CURTIS G. VIEBRANZ, JOSEPH J. WARD
Vice Presidents: STEPHEN L. BAIR, BONITA L. BOEZEMAN, STEPHEN L. GOLDSTEIN, JUANITA T. JAMES,
ANDREW P. KAPLAN, TREVOR LUNN, SUSAN J. MARUYAMA, ROBERT H. SMITH
Supervisor of Quality Control: JAMES KING
Publisher: JOSEPH J. WARD

For information about any Time-Life book please call 1-800-621-7026, or write:
Reader Information, Time-Life Customer Service
P.O. Box C-32068, Richmond, Virginia 23261-2068

Time-Life Books Inc. offers a wide range of fine recordings, including a Rock 'n' Roll Era series.
For subscription information, call 1-800-621-7026, or write TIME-LIFE MUSIC,
P.O. Box C-32068, Richmond, Virginia 23261-2068.